LLEWELLYN'S 2023

MOON SIGN

DATEBOOK

Weekly Planning by the Cycles of the Moon

Llewellyn's 2023 Moon Sign Datebook®

ISBN 978-0-7387-6398-9

Cover design by Kevin R. Brown
Editing by Hanna Grimson
Interior art by Caitlyn Barone on pages 11, 32, 59, 82, 128, 156; Kathleen Edwards on pages 16, 40, 68, 95, 142, 170; Wen Hsu on pages 30, 53, 73, 110, 137, 158

Typography owned by Llewellyn Worldwide Ltd.

Any internet references contained in this work are current at publication time, but the publisher cannot guarantee that a specific location will continue to be maintained.

Monthly moon-at-a-glance information written by Michelle Perrin. Astrological data compiled and programmed by Rique Pottenger. Based on the earlier work of Neil F. Michelsen. A special thanks to Beth Rosato for astrological proofreading.

You can order Llewellyn annuals and books from *New Worlds*, Llewellyn's catalog. To request a free copy of the catalog, call toll-free 1-877-NEW-WRLD or visit our website at www.llewellyn.com.

Llewellyn Publications
A Division of Llewellyn Worldwide Ltd.
2143 Wooddale Drive
Woodbury, MN 55125-2989
www.llewellyn.com

Printed in China

2023
Calendar
Pages

2023

January
S	M	T	W	T	F	S
1	2	3	4	5	6	7
8	9	10	11	12	13	14
15	16	17	18	19	20	21
22	23	24	25	26	27	28
29	30	31				

February
S	M	T	W	T	F	S
			1	2	3	4
5	6	7	8	9	10	11
12	13	14	15	16	17	18
19	20	21	22	23	24	25
26	27	28				

March
S	M	T	W	T	F	S
			1	2	3	4
5	6	7	8	9	10	11
12	13	14	15	16	17	18
19	20	21	22	23	24	25
26	27	28	29	30	31	

April
S	M	T	W	T	F	S
						1
2	3	4	5	6	7	8
9	10	11	12	13	14	15
16	17	18	19	20	21	22
23	24	25	26	27	28	29
30						

May
S	M	T	W	T	F	S
	1	2	3	4	5	6
7	8	9	10	11	12	13
14	15	16	17	18	19	20
21	22	23	24	25	26	27
28	29	30	31			

June
S	M	T	W	T	F	S
				1	2	3
4	5	6	7	8	9	10
11	12	13	14	15	16	17
18	19	20	21	22	23	24
25	26	27	28	29	30	

July
S	M	T	W	T	F	S
						1
2	3	4	5	6	7	8
9	10	11	12	13	14	15
16	17	18	19	20	21	22
23	24	25	26	27	28	29
30	31					

August
S	M	T	W	T	F	S
		1	2	3	4	5
6	7	8	9	10	11	12
13	14	15	16	17	18	19
20	21	22	23	24	25	26
27	28	29	30	31		

September
S	M	T	W	T	F	S
					1	2
3	4	5	6	7	8	9
10	11	12	13	14	15	16
17	18	19	20	21	22	23
24	25	26	27	28	29	30

October
S	M	T	W	T	F	S
1	2	3	4	5	6	7
8	9	10	11	12	13	14
15	16	17	18	19	20	21
22	23	24	25	26	27	28
29	30	31				

November
S	M	T	W	T	F	S
			1	2	3	4
5	6	7	8	9	10	11
12	13	14	15	16	17	18
19	20	21	22	23	24	25
26	27	28	29	30		

December
S	M	T	W	T	F	S
					1	2
3	4	5	6	7	8	9
10	11	12	13	14	15	16
17	18	19	20	21	22	23
24	25	26	27	28	29	30
31						

2024

January

S	M	T	W	T	F	S
	1	2	3	4	5	6
7	8	9	10	11	12	13
14	15	16	17	18	19	20
21	22	23	24	25	26	27
28	29	30	31			

February

S	M	T	W	T	F	S
				1	2	3
4	5	6	7	8	9	10
11	12	13	14	15	16	17
18	19	20	21	22	23	24
25	26	27	28	29		

March

S	M	T	W	T	F	S
					1	2
3	4	5	6	7	8	9
10	11	12	13	14	15	16
17	18	19	20	21	22	23
24	25	26	27	28	29	30
31						

April

S	M	T	W	T	F	S
	1	2	3	4	5	6
7	8	9	10	11	12	13
14	15	16	17	18	19	20
21	22	23	24	25	26	27
28	29	30				

May

S	M	T	W	T	F	S
			1	2	3	4
5	6	7	8	9	10	11
12	13	14	15	16	17	18
19	20	21	22	23	24	25
26	27	28	29	30	31	

June

S	M	T	W	T	F	S
						1
2	3	4	5	6	7	8
9	10	11	12	13	14	15
16	17	18	19	20	21	22
23	24	25	26	27	28	29
30						

July

S	M	T	W	T	F	S
	1	2	3	4	5	6
7	8	9	10	11	12	13
14	15	16	17	18	19	20
21	22	23	24	25	26	27
28	29	30	31			

August

S	M	T	W	T	F	S
				1	2	3
4	5	6	7	8	9	10
11	12	13	14	15	16	17
18	19	20	21	22	23	24
25	26	27	28	29	30	31

September

S	M	T	W	T	F	S
1	2	3	4	5	6	7
8	9	10	11	12	13	14
15	16	17	18	19	20	21
22	23	24	25	26	27	28
29	30					

October

S	M	T	W	T	F	S
		1	2	3	4	5
6	7	8	9	10	11	12
13	14	15	16	17	18	19
20	21	22	23	24	25	26
27	28	29	30	31		

November

S	M	T	W	T	F	S
					1	2
3	4	5	6	7	8	9
10	11	12	13	14	15	16
17	18	19	20	21	22	23
24	25	26	27	28	29	30

December

S	M	T	W	T	F	S
1	2	3	4	5	6	7
8	9	10	11	12	13	14
15	16	17	18	19	20	21
22	23	24	25	26	27	28
29	30	31				

2023 Moon Sign Datebook

Whether you have been a longtime reader of *Llewellyn's Moon Sign Book* or you are new to the rhythms of the Moon, you are now well on your way to achieving the rewards of weekly planning by the cycles of the Moon. Enjoy!

What You'll Find Inside

The clean, convenient space for planning and scheduling all your events and activities for the 2023 calendar year, the *Datebook* includes the daily Moon sign; New, Full, and quarter Moons; Moon void-of-course times; major US and UK holidays; and the best days for planting and fishing.

Inside you will also find informative content, Moon facts and lore, and everything you need to know about each month's New and Full Moons.

Void-of-Course Times

Void-of-course times are the periods of time when the Moon has left a given Moon sign but has yet to enter its next sign. At this time the Moon is void, and it is not considered a good time to initiate plans.

Gardening by the Moon

Talk to any traditional gardener or farmer and they will tell you specific Moon phases for doing chores. For example, prune trees and bushes to encourage growth when the Moon is going from new to full, and trim them to retard growth when the Moon is going from full to new. Plant root crops when the Moon is waning, and plant things that grow above ground when it is waxing. Pulling weeds and any work that involves clearing should be done during a waning Moon. Pick vegetables to preserve when the Moon is waxing, as it will draw the flavor into them.

For each month you will find detailed gardening instructions for each quarter Moon phase.

Monthly Moon at a Glance
By Michelle Perrin, Astrology Detective

The monthly "Moon at a Glance" sections throughout the Datebook are dedicated to the New and Full Moons for each month. Take note that this information sometimes appears at the beginning of a month and sometimes toward the end of the month. At the beginning of each month, flip through the weekly pages to locate and familiarize yourself with this lunar knowledge.

Moon 101: Remember the Basics

New Moon—New Beginnings: Things started at a New Moon have a great chance to bear the fruit of success over the next twelve months. Initiate projects and plant the seeds for new endeavors.

Full Moon—Good Goodbyes: If you are carrying around baggage, people, ideas, or habits that no longer suit you, you can shake them off for good at a Full Moon.

Eclipses—Shake Things Up: Sometimes we know what is best for ourselves yet cling to old ways out of fear or comfort. Eclipses come along to drag us kicking and screaming from our comfort zones. New Moon solar eclipses give us the courage to embrace the new, while Full Moon lunar eclipses get us out of bad, outworn situations.

Occultations—Like an Eclipse: Instead of being between the Sun and Moon, they are when the Moon aligns with a planet, temporarily blocking it from sight. Just like with solar and lunar eclipses, when a planet is occulted, its energy is being temporarily shut out and can go a bit haywire.

Lunar Phenomena

A Supermoon is when the Moon makes its closest approach to Earth and the center of the Moon is less than 223,694 miles from the center of Earth. Due to its nearness to the Earth, a Supermoon looks 7 percent wider and 15 percent brighter than a normal Moon.

The word "Supermoon" was first coined by the astrologer Richard Nolle in 1979. Astrologers traditionally called this phenomenon a "perigree."

A Micromoon is when the Moon is furthest from the Earth and looks smaller than usual. Traditionally, this is called an "apogee."

Blood Moons are named after their reddish hue. Blood Moons only happen at total lunar eclipses when the Moon blocks out the light of the Sun and only the Earth's light reaches it. Air molecules scatter out most of the blue light, leaving only red wavelengths to illuminate the lunar orb. Blood Moons are relatively rare, with the next one being in March 2025, and the previous one in May 2021.

A Black Moon refers to when there are two New Moons in one month. Alternatively, the third New Moon in a season with four New Moons is referred to as a Black Moon.

A Blue Moon is when a month has two Full Moons; the second one is known as a Blue Moon. A second definition is when a season has four Full Moons; the third is also called a Blue Moon.

For more specific details on the phases of the Moon, see Amy Herring's article, "The Eight Phases of the Moon," on page 182.

The Mysterious Moon
By Charlie Rainbow Wolf

It's easy to take the Moon for granted. Sometimes we notice it in the sky, but mostly we just assume that it's going to be there, doing whatever it is that it does. Some of you might wonder if the Moon actually does anything at all, apart from inspiring writers and artists and giving others ideas about space travel.

The Moon has been fascinating people forever. Prehistoric calendars from many different cultures reveal that early man tried to make sense of the solar and lunar cycles. Artists from all eras have celebrated the Moon phases, from the Paleolithic cave drawings in France, which date back some 15,000 years, right through to the present generation of painters who delight in the mystery of Earth's own satellite.

Lunar and Solar Eclipses

One of the most interesting things about the Moon has to do with the eclipses. There are two kinds, solar and lunar. They both occur at least twice a year, and they can both be partial or total. There can be as many as seven eclipses in a year, or as few as four. Total eclipses happen approximately every eighteen months—but of course, there are exceptions to every rule. Lunar eclipses happen when the shadow of the Earth covers the Moon. These only occur during a Full Moon.

History tells us that before all the science was understood, eclipses were feared by people, who believed that it was a sign from the gods. Of course, today the eclipses are predictable—but they're still pretty compelling. The Sun and the Moon are just the right size so, depending on the vantage point, when the Moon passes between the Sun and the Earth, it's the exact diameter to block out the Sun's light, no more, no less. This causes a total solar eclipse. We know that this is all part of the astronomical performance of these two lights, but that makes it no less fascinating.

On the Moon

In 1969, history was made when Neil Armstrong was the first man to ever set foot on the Moon. Along with Buzz Aldrin and Michael Collins, he collected rock samples and played golf and beamed back televised footage of their lunar landing. The rock samples—along with those later collected by subsequent Apollo missions, Soviet space exploration, and lunar meteorites—revealed that the Moon's composition is quite different than that of the Earth. The Moon rocks were low or missing in some familiar elements, with no evidence of hydration. Radiometric dating shows these rocks to be approximately 4.5 billion years old. Moon dust has proven to be older than Moon rocks, and they're both older than the Earth.

What Does the Moon Do?

Apart from being inspiration for poets, painters, and ponderers, the Moon actually does a lot to help sustain life on the third rock from the Sun. If it weren't for the Moon, the Earth would shift dramatically on its axis. The Moon's gravitational pull keeps the axis angled between 23 and 26 degrees, keeping the Earth's tilt disciplined and regulating the seasons. Without the Moon's assistance, seasons would be of unpredictable length and weather.

The ocean tides would be significantly less dramatic without the Moon's gravitational pull, too. They'd be governed by the Sun. The Sun is much larger than the Moon, but it is also much farther away. There would be no spring tide swell, no neap tides; in fact, there'd be very little tidal action at all! This would also influence the tidal animals, such as oysters, which open and shut in rhythm with the waters. Oysters have long been associated with this behavior. What makes them interesting is that if you move oysters inland, away from the coast, within a few days they'll alter their actions, and start to open and close with the movements of the Moon, not the tides.

It goes without saying that the nights would be much darker without the Moon. If you've ever marvelled at a starlit night when the Moon was dark, you'll get a bit of an idea as to just how the Moon lights up the sky. Not only that, though; the days on Earth would be a lot shorter without the Moon because of the way the Moon keeps the planet disciplined. Without the Moon, a day would only be six to eight hours long, and there would be over 1,000 days in a year! There would also be a larger equatorial bulge, and the area at the poles would be much flatter. The Moon really does do much more than just shine a light in the night sky!

Why Is the Moon So Fascinating?

It's not just all the astronomy that seduces people when it comes to the Moon, though. EMS workers have noticed a rise in activity when the Moon is full. There are all kinds of old wives' tales about a woman's menstrual cycle being in rhythm with the phases of the Moon and that babies are more likely to be born during a Full Moon than any other time. While some of these have been disproven over the years, other lunar trivia does hold water.

It's not just those living close to the land who use the phases of the Moon to get the most out of things, though. Business people who are aware of the lunar influences will schedule meetings as the Moon is waxing in order to bring people together. Beauticians will trim hair and nails according to the lunar phases to either encourage or discourage growth. Each of the Moon's phases will bring with it a particular energy, and working in harmony with those energies helps make the most of a particular task or activity.

There are nocturnal activities where the light of the Moon—or lack of it—might be preferred. For example, hunters have observed that their nighttime prey is more animated during a Full Moon than a darker one. Fishermen also pay attention to the Moon's pull on the tides and use it to their advantage when casting off. Convicted burglars have divulged that they prefer to work when the skies are dark.

Perhaps it's the subdued light and the increase in some behaviors that has made moonlight so popular with writers, dabblers, musicians, and other artists. In the half-light of the Moon, illusions can be easily woven. What was a shadow by day might be seen as a terrifying monster at night; what was mundane in the sunlight could turn into a beauty by moonlight. The Moon charms, enthralls, and mesmerizes even the most practical of persons. Paintings like Van Gogh's *Starry Night*, songs like "Blue Moon" by Richard Rodgers, and universal myths—such as the one about the Moon being made of cheese—stand as testimony that the love affair with the Moon is enduring.

2023 Eclipses

Solar Eclipse	April 20	29°	♈	50'
Lunar Eclipse	May 5	14°	♏	58'
Solar Eclipse	October 14	21°	♎	08'
Lunar Eclipse	October 28	5°	♉	09'

Equinoxes and Solstices

Spring Equinox	March 20
Summer Solstice	June 21
Fall Equinox	September 23
Winter Solstice	December 21

Mercury Retrograde

Mercury Retrograde	12/29/22	4:32 am	Direct	1/18	8:12 am
Mercury Retrograde	4/21	4:35 am	Direct	5/14	11:17 pm
Mercury Retrograde	8/23	3:59 pm	Direct	9/15	4:21 pm
Mercury Retrograde	12/13	2:09 am	Direct	1/1/24	10:08 pm

Signs:

♈	Aries	♌	Leo	♐	Sagittarius
♉	Taurus	♍	Virgo	♑	Capricorn
♊	Gemini	♎	Libra	♒	Aquarius
♋	Cancer	♏	Scorpio	♓	Pisces

Phases:

New Moon: ●   Best Days for Planting: 🌱

2nd Quarter: ◑

Full Moon: ○   Best Days for Fishing: 🐟

4th Quarter: ◐

V/C: Void of Course

January

January 2023

Sun	Mon	Tue	Wed
1 New Year's Day	2	3	4
8	9	10	11
15	16 Martin Luther King Jr. Day	17	18
22	23	24	25
29	30	31	1
5	6	7	8

Set in Eastern Standard Time (EST)

Thu	Fri	Sat	
5	○ 6	7	*Notes*
12	13	◐ 14	
19	20	● 21	
26	27	◐ 28	
2	3	4	
9	10	11	

2023 Occultation Guide

This year, there are twelve occultations of the visible planets, Mercury through Jupiter.

Occultation of Mercury: October 14. Thinking will be cloudy on this day, leading to dubious decision-making and poor planning. It's better to put off any major choices until this energy has passed.

Occultation of Venus: March 24 and November 9. Emotional vampires wander the earth during these periods, seeking to unload their neediness and perpetual victimhood on unwitting prey. Try to keep your wits about you to avoid being guilt-tripped or manipulated into picking up other people's responsibilities. Feelings can easily be hurt, and diplomacy goes haywire, so it's best to adopt a detached attitude.

Occultation of Mars: January 4, January 31, February 28, September 17, and October 16. On these dates, anger runs high, causing disputes to erupt over highly trivial matters. Physical energy levels could also run low, so it's best to rest and stay off the radar of difficult people. Put off delicate negotiations or discussions to another day.

Occultation of Jupiter: February 23, March 23, April 20, and May 17. Jupiter drops a nuclear bomb on whatever it touches. Things could be blown out of proportion in all aspects of life. Fights may break out, or there could be a tendency to overspend. Alternatively, you could come up with the world's absolute greatest idea that is actually completely misguided and off the mark. Egos are inflated, so beware of unctuous flattery or feeling insulted when people don't bow at your feet. Try to rein things in.

Set in Eastern Standard Time (EST)

January's Moon at a Glance

January 6 Full Moon/Micromoon
Forget the Past

It's the new year and time for new beginnings, free of the baggage of the past. Compulsively dwelling over past hurts could keep wounds from truly healing. If you find yourself obsessing over prior pain, try to become consciously aware that it happened long ago, and you are in a place of safety now.

January 21 New Moon
Bright-Eyed and Bushy-Tailed

This super-energetic New Moon is bursting with enthusiastic, positive energy. Try to break boundaries and dare to embark on unknown adventures. It will be easy to wander beyond your comfort zone, making this an excellent time to launch projects and reach out to new connections.

Sunday 1
2nd ♉
New Year's Day
Kwanzaa ends

December '22						
S	M	T	W	T	F	S
				1	2	3
4	5	6	7	8	9	10
11	12	13	14	15	16	17
18	19	20	21	22	23	24
25	26	27	28	29	30	31

January						
S	M	T	W	T	F	S
1	2	3	4	5	6	7
8	9	10	11	12	13	14
15	16	17	18	19	20	21
22	23	24	25	26	27	28
29	30	31				

February						
S	M	T	W	T	F	S
			1	2	3	4
5	6	7	8	9	10	11
12	13	14	15	16	17	18
19	20	21	22	23	24	25
26	27	28				

January 2023

2 Monday
2nd
☽ v/c 5:16 pm
☽ enters ♊ 9:44 pm
Bank holiday (UK)

3 Tuesday
2nd ♊

4 Wednesday
2nd ♊
☽ v/c 7:08 pm

5 Thursday
2nd ♊
☽ enters ♋ 9:15 am

 ⟡

Set in Eastern Standard Time (EST)

Friday 6

2nd ♋

Full Moon 6:08 pm

Saturday 7

3rd ♋

☽ v/c 5:23 pm

☽ enters ♌ 9:40 pm

Sunday 8

3rd ♌

December '22						
S	M	T	W	T	F	S
				1	2	3
4	5	6	7	8	9	10
11	12	13	14	15	16	17
18	19	20	21	22	23	24
25	26	27	28	29	30	31

January						
S	M	T	W	T	F	S
1	2	3	4	5	6	7
8	9	10	11	12	13	14
15	16	17	18	19	20	21
22	23	24	25	26	27	28
29	30	31				

February						
S	M	T	W	T	F	S
			1	2	3	4
5	6	7	8	9	10	11
12	13	14	15	16	17	18
19	20	21	22	23	24	25
26	27	28				

9 Monday
3rd ♌︎
☽ v/c 8:52 pm

10 Tuesday
3rd ♌︎
☽ enters ♍︎ 10:15 am

11 Wednesday
3rd ♍︎

12 Thursday
3rd ♍︎
☽ v/c 6:06 pm
☽ enters ♎︎ 9:56 pm

Friday 13

3rd ♎

Saturday 14

3rd ♎

4th Quarter 9:10 pm

Sunday 15

4th ♎

☽ v/c 3:40 am

☽ enters ♏ 7:08 am

December '22						
S	M	T	W	T	F	S
				1	2	3
4	5	6	7	8	9	10
11	12	13	14	15	16	17
18	19	20	21	22	23	24
25	26	27	28	29	30	31

January						
S	M	T	W	T	F	S
1	2	3	4	5	6	7
8	9	10	11	12	13	14
15	16	17	18	19	20	21
22	23	24	25	26	27	28
29	30	31				

February						
S	M	T	W	T	F	S
			1	2	3	4
5	6	7	8	9	10	11
12	13	14	15	16	17	18
19	20	21	22	23	24	25
26	27	28				

---

16 Monday
4th ♏

Martin Luther King Jr. Day

---

17 Tuesday
4th ♏

☽ v/c 9:27 am

☽ enters ♐ 12:33 pm

---

18 Wednesday
4th ♐

Mercury direct 8:12 am

---

19 Thursday
4th ♐

☽ v/c 5:09 am

☽ enters ♑ 2:11 pm

Friday 20

4th ♑

Saturday 21

4th ♑

☽ v/c 10:52 am

☽ enters ♒ 1:29 pm

New Moon 3:53 pm

Sunday 22

1st ♒

Lunar New Year

December '22

S	M	T	W	T	F	S
				1	2	3
4	5	6	7	8	9	10
11	12	13	14	15	16	17
18	19	20	21	22	23	24
25	26	27	28	29	30	31

January

S	M	T	W	T	F	S
1	2	3	4	5	6	7
8	9	10	11	12	13	14
15	16	17	18	19	20	21
22	23	24	25	26	27	28
29	30	31				

February

S	M	T	W	T	F	S
			1	2	3	4
5	6	7	8	9	10	11
12	13	14	15	16	17	18
19	20	21	22	23	24	25
26	27	28				

---

23 Monday

1st ≈
☽ v/c 5:19 am
☽ enters ♓ 12:36 pm

---

24 Tuesday

1st ♓

---

25 Wednesday

1st ♓
☽ v/c 11:12 am
☽ enters ♈ 1:48 pm

---

26 Thursday

1st ♈

Friday 27

1st ♈

☽ v/c 4:01 pm

☽ enters ♉ 6:42 pm

Saturday 28

1st ♉

2nd Quarter 10:19 am

Sunday 29

2nd ♉

December '22						
S	M	T	W	T	F	S
				1	2	3
4	5	6	7	8	9	10
11	12	13	14	15	16	17
18	19	20	21	22	23	24
25	26	27	28	29	30	31

January						
S	M	T	W	T	F	S
1	2	3	4	5	6	7
8	9	10	11	12	13	14
15	16	17	18	19	20	21
22	23	24	25	26	27	28
29	30	31				

February						
S	M	T	W	T	F	S
			1	2	3	4
5	6	7	8	9	10	11
12	13	14	15	16	17	18
19	20	21	22	23	24	25
26	27	28				

January 2023

30 Monday
2nd ♉

☽ v/c 12:52 am

☽ enters ♊ 3:35 am

31 Tuesday
2nd ♊

In the Garden
Jan. 6, 6:08 pm–Jan. 7, 9:40 pm (3rd ♋): Plant biennials, perennials, bulbs and roots. Prune. Irrigate. Fertilize (organic).

Jan. 15, 7:08 am–Jan. 17, 12:33 pm (4th ♏): Plant biennials, perennials, bulbs and roots. Prune. Irrigate. Fertilize (organic).

Jan. 23, 12:36 pm–Jan. 25, 1:48 pm (1st ♓): Plant grains, leafy annuals. Fertilize (chemical). Graft or bud plants. Irrigate. Trim to increase growth.

Jan. 28, 10:19 am–Jan. 30, 3:35 am (2nd ♉): Plant annuals for hardiness. Trim to increase growth.

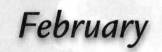

February

February 2023

Sun	Mon	Tue	Wed
			1
○ 5	6	7	8
12	◑ 13	14 Valentine's Day	15
19	● 20 Presidents' Day	21	22
26	◐ 27	28	1
5	6	7	8

Set in Eastern Standard Time (EST)

Thu	Fri	Sat	Notes
2 Groundhog Day	3	4	_____ _____ _____ _____
9	10	11	_____ _____ _____ _____
16	17	18	_____ _____ _____ _____
23	24	25	_____ _____ _____ _____
2	3	4	_____ _____ _____ _____
9	10	11	_____ _____

New Moon on Monday

In honor of this month's New Moon on Monday, we take a trip down memory lane to one of Duran Duran's catchiest tunes— and also the video the group dislikes the most. According to the band's former lead guitarist, Andy Taylor, he cringes any time he sees the video for the band's 1984 hit single "New Moon on Monday," especially when they are all dancing at the end. The video was filmed in the medieval French town of Noyers, near Dijon, in the dead of winter in January 1984. It was so cold at night, the band had to drink to keep warm. By the time they shot the final scenes, they were completely drunk. It was one of the only times Taylor ever saw keyboardist Nick Rhodes dance.

The video features the Fab Five joined by 1980's Miss France, Patricia Barzyk, portraying members of an underground, resistance-style group. Since much of the video has lead singer, Simon Le Bon, riding behind the female protagonist on the back of a motorcycle, Barzyk assured the director she knew how to drive one when she auditioned for the part. Once they got to the set, however, it became evident she didn't. Luckily, the crew's gaffer stepped in and saved the day, and you can still make out his masculine face behind the visor in the scene where they arrive in town.

February's Moon at a Glance

February 5 Full Moon/Micromoon
Rebel Yell

Everyone will be up for a fight under this highly emotional Full Moon. Hypocrisy will be called out immediately, as no one will be willing to play the game or keep up appearances merely for the sake of social propriety. Stand up for your rights, but realize that all battlefields bear scars once the fighting is over.

February 20 New Moon
The Hermit

This New Moon stands alone next to Saturn, cut off from making connections to any other planets in the chart. This is a good moment for finding wisdom through introspection and solitary pursuits. Try to tap into the meaning from within instead of seeking validation from the outside world.

In the Garden

Feb. 5, 1:29 pm–Feb. 6, 4:14 pm (3rd ♌): Cultivate. Destroy weeds and pests. Harvest fruits and root crops for food. Trim to retard growth.

Feb. 13, 11:01 am–Feb. 13, 8:31 pm (4th ♏): Plant biennials, perennials, bulbs and roots. Prune. Irrigate. Fertilize (organic).

Feb. 20, 2:06–Feb. 22, 12:14 am (1st ♓): Plant grains, leafy annuals. Fertilize (chemical). Graft or bud plants. Irrigate. Trim to increase growth.

Feb. 28, 9:40 pm–Mar. 3, 10:16 am (2nd ♋): Plant grains, leafy annuals. Fertilize (chemical). Graft or bud plants. Irrigate. Trim to increase growth.

---

1 Wednesday

2nd ♊

☽ v/c 6:58 am

☽ enters ♋ 3:11 pm

---

2 Thursday

2nd ♋

Groundhog Day

Friday 3

2nd

☽ v/c 10:19 pm

Saturday 4

2nd ♋

☽ v/c 1:19 am

☽ enters ♌ 3:48 am

Sunday 5

2nd ♌

Full Moon 1:29 pm

	January					
S	M	T	W	T	F	S
1	2	3	4	5	6	7
8	9	10	11	12	13	14
15	16	17	18	19	20	21
22	23	24	25	26	27	28
29	30	31				

	February					
S	M	T	W	T	F	S
			1	2	3	4
5	6	7	8	9	10	11
12	13	14	15	16	17	18
19	20	21	22	23	24	25
26	27	28				

	March					
S	M	T	W	T	F	S
			1	2	3	4
5	6	7	8	9	10	11
12	13	14	15	16	17	18
19	20	21	22	23	24	25
26	27	28	29	30	31	

February 2023

6 Monday
3rd ♌
☽ v/c 9:15 am
☽ enters ♍ 4:14 pm

7 Tuesday
3rd ♍

8 Wednesday
3rd ♍

9 Thursday
3rd ♍
☽ v/c 1:40 am
☽ enters ♎ 3:47 am

Set in Eastern Standard Time (EST)

Friday 10
3rd ♎

Saturday 11
3rd ♎

☽ v/c 11:41 am
☽ enters ♏ 1:34 pm

Sunday 12
3rd ♏

			January			
S	M	T	W	T	F	S
1	2	3	4	5	6	7
8	9	10	11	12	13	14
15	16	17	18	19	20	21
22	23	24	25	26	27	28
29	30	31				

			February			
S	M	T	W	T	F	S
			1	2	3	4
5	6	7	8	9	10	11
12	13	14	15	16	17	18
19	20	21	22	23	24	25
26	27	28				

			March			
S	M	T	W	T	F	S
			1	2	3	4
5	6	7	8	9	10	11
12	13	14	15	16	17	18
19	20	21	22	23	24	25
26	27	28	29	30	31	

February 2023

13 Monday
3rd
4th Quarter 11:01 am
☽ v/c 6:52 pm
☽ enters ♐ 8:31 pm

14 Tuesday
4th ♐
Valentine's Day

15 Wednesday
4th ♐
☽ v/c 8:06 pm

16 Thursday
4th ♑
☽ enters ♑ 12:00 am

Friday 17

4th ♑

☽ v/c 11:18 pm

Saturday 18

4th ♑

☽ enters ♒ 12:35 am

Sunday 19

4th ♒

☽ v/c 9:00 pm

☽ enters ♓ 11:56 pm

	January					
S	M	T	W	T	F	S
1	2	3	4	5	6	7
8	9	10	11	12	13	14
15	16	17	18	19	20	21
22	23	24	25	26	27	28
29	30	31				

	February					
S	M	T	W	T	F	S
			1	2	3	4
5	6	7	8	9	10	11
12	13	14	15	16	17	18
19	20	21	22	23	24	25
26	27	28				

	March					
S	M	T	W	T	F	S
			1	2	3	4
5	6	7	8	9	10	11
12	13	14	15	16	17	18
19	20	21	22	23	24	25
26	27	28	29	30	31	

20 Monday
4th ♓
New Moon 2:06 am
Presidents' Day

21 Tuesday
1st ♓
☽ v/c 11:06 pm
Mardi Gras (Fat Tuesday)

22 Wednesday
1st ♓
☽ enters ♈ 12:14 am
Ash Wednesday

23 Thursday
1st ♈

February 2023

Friday 24

1st ♈

☽ v/c 2:22 am

☽ enters ♉ 3:29 am

Saturday 25

1st ♉

Sunday 26

1st ♉

☽ v/c 9:42 am

☽ enters ♊ 10:48 am

January						
S	M	T	W	T	F	S
1	2	3	4	5	6	7
8	9	10	11	12	13	14
15	16	17	18	19	20	21
22	23	24	25	26	27	28
29	30	31				

February						
S	M	T	W	T	F	S
			1	2	3	4
5	6	7	8	9	10	11
12	13	14	15	16	17	18
19	20	21	22	23	24	25
26	27	28				

March						
S	M	T	W	T	F	S
			1	2	3	4
5	6	7	8	9	10	11
12	13	14	15	16	17	18
19	20	21	22	23	24	25
26	27	28	29	30	31	

February 2023

27 Monday

1st ♊

2nd Quarter 3:06 am

28 Tuesday

2nd ♊

☽ v/c 8:07 pm

☽ enters ♋ 9:40 pm

Set in Eastern Standard Time (EST)

March

March 2023

Sun	Mon	Tue	Wed
			1
5	6	○ 7	8
12 Daylight Saving Time begins	13	◐ 14	15
19	20	● 21	22
26	27	◑ 28	29
2	3	4	5

Set in Eastern Standard Time (EST)

Thu	Fri	Sat	Notes
2	3	4	
9	10	11	
16	17	18	
	St. Patrick's Day		
23	24	25	
30	31	1	
6	7	8	

March's Moon at a Glance

March 7 Full Moon

Get It All Out

If you have been harboring suspicions or paranoia about the people around you, instead of mulling things over incessantly in your mind, it's time for a confrontation. Only by clearing the air will you be able to accurately assess the situation and come to a proper conclusion.

March 21 New Moon

Just Say No

If you are being bulldozed into making a decision or acting against your own inner compass, it's time to stand up to peer pressure and hold your ground. This Moon is filled with competition, envy, and rivalry. Refuse to play the game and, instead, focus on your own goals.

---

1 Wednesday

2nd ♋

St. David's Day (Wales)

---

2 Thursday

2nd ♋

Friday 3
2nd ♋
☽ v/c 9:22 am
☽ enters ♌ 10:16 am

Saturday 4
2nd ♌

Sunday 5
2nd ♌
☽ v/c 10:18 pm
☽ enters ♍ 10:38 pm

February						
S	M	T	W	T	F	S
			1	2	3	4
5	6	7	8	9	10	11
12	13	14	15	16	17	18
19	20	21	22	23	24	25
26	27	28				

March						
S	M	T	W	T	F	S
			1	2	3	4
5	6	7	8	9	10	11
12	13	14	15	16	17	18
19	20	21	22	23	24	25
26	27	28	29	30	31	

April						
S	M	T	W	T	F	S
						1
2	3	4	5	6	7	8
9	10	11	12	13	14	15
16	17	18	19	20	21	22
23	24	25	26	27	28	29
30						

March 2023

6 Monday
2nd ♍

Purim begins at sundown

7 Tuesday
2nd ♍

Full Moon 7:40 am

8 Wednesday
3rd ♍

☽ v/c 9:07 am

☽ enters ♎ 9:44 am

9 Thursday
3rd ♎

Friday 10

3rd ♎

☽ v/c 6:37 pm

☽ enters ♏ 7:06 pm

Saturday 11

3rd ♏

Sunday 12

3rd ♏

Daylight Saving Time begins at 2 am

February						
S	M	T	W	T	F	S
			1	2	3	4
5	6	7	8	9	10	11
12	13	14	15	16	17	18
19	20	21	22	23	24	25
26	27	28				

March						
S	M	T	W	T	F	S
			1	2	3	4
5	6	7	8	9	10	11
12	13	14	15	16	17	18
19	20	21	22	23	24	25
26	27	28	29	30	31	

April						
S	M	T	W	T	F	S
						1
2	3	4	5	6	7	8
9	10	11	12	13	14	15
16	17	18	19	20	21	22
23	24	25	26	27	28	29
30						

March 2023

13 Monday
3rd ♏
☽ v/c 2:58 am
☽ enters ♐ 3:21 am
Commonwealth Day (UK)

14 Tuesday
3rd ♐
4th Quarter 10:08 pm

15 Wednesday
4th ♐
☽ v/c 4:50 am
☽ enters ♑ 8:06 am

16 Thursday
4th ♑

Friday 17

4th ♑

☽ v/c 10:14 am

☽ enters ♒ 10:25 am

St. Patrick's Day

Saturday 18

4th ♒

Sunday 19

4th ♒

☽ v/c 6:33 am

☽ enters ♓ 11:12 am

Mothering Sunday (UK)

	February					
S	M	T	W	T	F	S
			1	2	3	4
5	6	7	8	9	10	11
12	13	14	15	16	17	18
19	20	21	22	23	24	25
26	27	28				

	March					
S	M	T	W	T	F	S
			1	2	3	4
5	6	7	8	9	10	11
12	13	14	15	16	17	18
19	20	21	22	23	24	25
26	27	28	29	30	31	

	April					
S	M	T	W	T	F	S
						1
2	3	4	5	6	7	8
9	10	11	12	13	14	15
16	17	18	19	20	21	22
23	24	25	26	27	28	29
30						

March 2023

---

20 Monday

4th ♓

Spring Equinox

---

21 Tuesday

4th ♓

☽ v/c 11:58 am

☽ enters ♈ 12:01 pm

New Moon 1:23 pm

---

22 Wednesday

1st ♈

Ramadan begins at sundown

---

23 Thursday

1st ♈

☽ v/c 1:13 pm

☽ enters ♉ 2:42 pm

Set in Eastern Daylight Time (EDT)

Friday 24

1st ♉

Saturday 25

1st ♉

☽ v/c 12:19 pm

☽ enters ♊ 8:42 pm

Sunday 26

1st ♊

British Summer Time begins at 1 am

	February							March							April					
S	M	T	W	T	F	S	S	M	T	W	T	F	S	S	M	T	W	T	F	S
			1	2	3	4				1	2	3	4							1
5	6	7	8	9	10	11	5	6	7	8	9	10	11	2	3	4	5	6	7	8
12	13	14	15	16	17	18	12	13	14	15	16	17	18	9	10	11	12	13	14	15
19	20	21	22	23	24	25	19	20	21	22	23	24	25	16	17	18	19	20	21	22
26	27	28					26	27	28	29	30	31		23	24	25	26	27	28	29
														30						

March 2023

---

27 Monday

1st ♊

☽ v/c 9:39 pm

---

28 Tuesday

1st ♊

☽ enters ♋ 6:22 am

2nd Quarter 10:32 pm

---

29 Wednesday

2nd ♋

---

30 Thursday

2nd ♋

☽ v/c 9:45 am

☽ enters ♌ 6:31 pm

Set in Eastern Daylight Time (EDT)

Friday 31
2nd ♌

February						
S	M	T	W	T	F	S
			1	2	3	4
5	6	7	8	9	10	11
12	13	14	15	16	17	18
19	20	21	22	23	24	25
26	27	28				

March						
S	M	T	W	T	F	S
			1	2	3	4
5	6	7	8	9	10	11
12	13	14	15	16	17	18
19	20	21	22	23	24	25
26	27	28	29	30	31	

April						
S	M	T	W	T	F	S
						1
2	3	4	5	6	7	8
9	10	11	12	13	14	15
16	17	18	19	20	21	22
23	24	25	26	27	28	29
30						

The Norse God of the Moon

In Norse mythology, the Moon god is named Máni, whose name is the basis for the word Monday. This male deity is the brother of the female Sun goddess, Sól. According to the *Prose Edda* written by Snorri Sturluson in the thirteenth century, these two siblings were considered so luminously beautiful by their father that he named them "Sun" and "Moon." Affronted by such arrogance, the gods snatched the two children and placed them in the heavens to drive the horse-drawn chariots of the Moon and Sun. They were incessantly chased by the wolves Skoll ("Mockery") and Hati ("Hate"), who threatened to swallow them. Lunar eclipses were thought to occur whenever Skoll got too close to the Moon. Máni was accompanied through the sky by two child-spirits, Bil and Hjuki, who he had snatched while they were out gathering water for their father. Both children are depicted carrying water and are associated with the waxing and waning of the Moon. Bil and Hjuki are believed to be the origin of the nursery rhyme "Jack and Jill."

In the Garden

Mar. 7, 7:40 am–Mar. 8, 9:44 am (3rd ♍): Cultivate, especially medicinal plants. Destroy weeds and pests. Trim to retard growth.

Mar. 14, 10:08 pm–Mar. 15, 8:06 am (4th ♐): Cultivate. Destroy weeds and pests. Harvest fruits and root crops for food. Trim to retard growth.

Mar. 23, 2:42 pm–Mar. 25, 8:42 pm (1st ♉): Plant annuals for hardiness. Trim to increase growth.

Mar. 28, 10:32 pm–Mar. 30, 6:31 pm (2nd ♋): Plant grains, leafy annuals. Fertilize (chemical). Graft or bud plants. Irrigate. Trim to increase growth.

April

April 2023

Sun	Mon	Tue	Wed
2	3	4	5
9 Easter	10	11	12
16	17	18	19
23	24	25	26
30	1	2	3

Set in Eastern Daylight Time (EDT)

Thu	Fri	Sat	Notes
		1 April Fools' Day	
○ 6	7 Good Friday	8	
◐ 13	14	15	
● 20	21	22	
◑ 27	28	29	
4	5	6	

This Year's Eclipse Guide

There are four eclipses this year: two lunar and two solar. A lunar eclipse happens at the Full Moon, when the Sun opposes the Moon, while a solar eclipse occurs at a New Moon, when the Sun and Moon are conjunct.

Eclipses always occur in pairs. The first set of eclipses will be in April and May and the second in October.

The first eclipse of the year will be a total solar eclipse on April 20. It can best be viewed in northwestern Australia and the islands between Australia and Southeast Asia, including Indonesia, East Timor, Guam, Micronesia, and New Guinea.

The penumbral lunar eclipse of May 5 can be viewed in Africa, Europe (excluding the British Isles), Australia, the South Pacific, and Asia.

The solar eclipse on October 14 is annular. It will be visible in the western United States, including Oregon, Utah, Nevada, New Mexico, and Texas, along with parts of California, Idaho, Colorado, and Arizona. It can also be viewed from Mexico's Yucatán Peninsula, Belize, Honduras, Panama, Colombia, and northern Brazil.

The year's final eclipse is a partial lunar eclipse on October 28. The eclipse can be fully viewed in Europe, Africa, Asia, central and western Australia, Greenland, and the easternmost part of Brazil.

In the Garden

Apr. 7, 2:29 am–Apr. 9, 8:57 am (3rd ♏): Plant biennials, perennials, bulbs and roots. Prune. Irrigate. Fertilize (organic).

Apr. 13, 5:11 am–Apr. 13, 4:42 pm (4th ♑): Plant potatoes and tubers. Trim to retard growth.

Apr. 20, 12:30 am–Apr. 22, 6:11 am (1st ♉): Plant annuals for hardiness. Trim to increase growth.

Saturday 1

2nd ♌

April Fools' Day

Sunday 2

2nd ♌

☽ v/c 2:03 am

☽ enters ♍ 6:57 am

Palm Sunday

	March					
S	M	T	W	T	F	S
			1	2	3	4
5	6	7	8	9	10	11
12	13	14	15	16	17	18
19	20	21	22	23	24	25
26	27	28	29	30	31	

	April					
S	M	T	W	T	F	S
						1
2	3	4	5	6	7	8
9	10	11	12	13	14	15
16	17	18	19	20	21	22
23	24	25	26	27	28	29
30						

	May					
S	M	T	W	T	F	S
	1	2	3	4	5	6
7	8	9	10	11	12	13
14	15	16	17	18	19	20
21	22	23	24	25	26	27
28	29	30	31			

April 2023

3 Monday
2nd ♍

4 Tuesday
2nd ♍

☽ v/c 9:50 am

☽ enters ♎ 5:51 pm

5 Wednesday
2nd ♎

Passover begins at sundown

6 Thursday
2nd ♎

Full Moon 12:34 am

☽ v/c 8:43 am

Set in Eastern Daylight Time (EDT)

Friday 7

3rd ♎

☽ enters ♏ 2:29 am

Good Friday

Saturday 8

3rd ♏

Sunday 9

3rd ♏

☽ v/c 5:09 am

☽ enters ♐ 8:57 am

Easter

	March								April								May					
S	M	T	W	T	F	S		S	M	T	W	T	F	S		S	M	T	W	T	F	S
			1	2	3	4								1			1	2	3	4	5	6
5	6	7	8	9	10	11		2	3	4	5	6	7	8		7	8	9	10	11	12	13
12	13	14	15	16	17	18		9	10	11	12	13	14	15		14	15	16	17	18	19	20
19	20	21	22	23	24	25		16	17	18	19	20	21	22		21	22	23	24	25	26	27
26	27	28	29	30	31			23	24	25	26	27	28	29		28	29	30	31			
								30														

April 2023

10 Monday
3rd ♐

Easter Monday (UK)

11 Tuesday
3rd ♐

☽ v/c 6:48 am

☽ enters ♑ 1:33 pm

12 Wednesday
3rd ♑

13 Thursday
3rd ♑

4th Quarter 5:11 am

☽ v/c 10:14 am

☽ enters ♒ 4:42 pm

Passover ends

Set in Eastern Daylight Time (EDT)

Friday 14

4th ≈

Orthodox Good Friday

Saturday 15

4th ≈

☽ v/c 11:16 am

☽ enters ♓ 6:57 pm

Sunday 16

4th ♓

Orthodox Easter

		March				
S	M	T	W	T	F	S
			1	2	3	4
5	6	7	8	9	10	11
12	13	14	15	16	17	18
19	20	21	22	23	24	25
26	27	28	29	30	31	

		April				
S	M	T	W	T	F	S
						1
2	3	4	5	6	7	8
9	10	11	12	13	14	15
16	17	18	19	20	21	22
23	24	25	26	27	28	29
30						

		May				
S	M	T	W	T	F	S
	1	2	3	4	5	6
7	8	9	10	11	12	13
14	15	16	17	18	19	20
21	22	23	24	25	26	27
28	29	30	31			

17 Monday

4th ♓

☽ v/c 2:57 pm

☽ enters ♈ 9:09 pm

18 Tuesday

4th ♈

19 Wednesday

4th ♈

20 Thursday

4th ♈

☽ v/c 12:13 am

New Moon 12:13 am

☽ enters ♉ 12:30 am

Solar eclipse

Friday 21

1st ♉

☽ v/c 11:41 pm

Ramadan ends

Mercury retrograde 4:35 am until 5/14

Saturday 22

1st ♉

☽ enters ♊ 6:11 am

Earth Day

Sunday 23

1st ♊

St. George's Day (England)

	March					
S	M	T	W	T	F	S
			1	2	3	4
5	6	7	8	9	10	11
12	13	14	15	16	17	18
19	20	21	22	23	24	25
26	27	28	29	30	31	

	April					
S	M	T	W	T	F	S
						1
2	3	4	5	6	7	8
9	10	11	12	13	14	15
16	17	18	19	20	21	22
23	24	25	26	27	28	29
30						

	May					
S	M	T	W	T	F	S
	1	2	3	4	5	6
7	8	9	10	11	12	13
14	15	16	17	18	19	20
21	22	23	24	25	26	27
28	29	30	31			

April 2023

---

24 Monday
1st ♊
☽ v/c 8:15 am
☽ enters ♋ 2:58 pm

---

25 Tuesday
1st ♋

---

26 Wednesday
1st ♋
☽ v/c 7:41 pm

---

27 Thursday
1st ♋
☽ enters ♌ 2:30 am
2nd Quarter 5:20 pm

Set in Eastern Daylight Time (EDT)

Friday 28
2nd ♌

Saturday 29
2nd ♌
☽ v/c 6:53 am
☽ enters ♍ 2:59 pm

Sunday 30
2nd ♍

	March							April							May					
S	M	T	W	T	F	S	S	M	T	W	T	F	S	S	M	T	W	T	F	S
			1	2	3	4							1		1	2	3	4	5	6
5	6	7	8	9	10	11	2	3	4	5	6	7	8	7	8	9	10	11	12	13
12	13	14	15	16	17	18	9	10	11	12	13	14	15	14	15	16	17	18	19	20
19	20	21	22	23	24	25	16	17	18	19	20	21	22	21	22	23	24	25	26	27
26	27	28	29	30	31		23	24	25	26	27	28	29	28	29	30	31			
							30													

April's Moon at a Glance

April 6 Full Moon

Ego Trip

The only thing standing in your way is your own inflated sense of self. Egos are a-popping all around, creating a scenario where everyone feels they are the second coming of Leonardo da Vinci, yet no one wants to actually pick up a paintbrush. The one who works humbly and diligently behind the scenes will end up winning the acclaim.

April 20 New Moon Total Solar Eclipse

Tall Poppy Syndrome

If you insist on standing out, don't be surprised if you become a target for jealous, envious competitors who want to cut you down. It may be better to fly under the radar and focus on directly impressing those who hold true power behind the scenes, so you can shoot to success without your rivals even realizing it.

Set in Eastern Daylight Time (EDT)

May

May 2023

Sun	Mon	Tue	Wed
	1	2	3
7	8	9	10
14 Mother's Day	15	16	17
21	22	23	24
28	29 Memorial Day	30	31
4	5	6	7

Set in Eastern Daylight Time (EDT)

Thu	Fri	Sat	
4	5 ○	6	**Notes**
			_____
			_____
			_____
11	12 ◑	13	_____
			_____
			_____
			_____
18	19 ●	20	_____
			_____
			_____
			_____
25	26	27 ◑	_____
			_____
			_____
			_____
1	2	3	_____
			_____
			_____
			_____
8	9	10	_____
			_____
			_____

May's Moon at a Glance

May 5 Full Moon Penumbral Lunar Eclipse
Throw Caution to the Wind

This eclipse is here to violently shake us out of negative thought patterns that create an overly cautious approach to life. We get only one life to live, and this is a moment for courage, adventure, and proceeding valiantly into the unknown so that life can surprise us with its hidden opportunities.

May 19 New Moon/Black Moon
Bold and Brave

This is an excellent time to go after your true innermost dreams. If you have a project sitting on the shelf gathering dust, this is the moment to bring your talents and expertise to the world so the entire universe can be elevated to a higher vibration.

In the Garden

May 2, 2:09 am–May 4, 10:32 am (2nd ♎): Plant annuals for fragrance and beauty. Trim to increase growth.

May 5, 1:34 pm–May 6, 4:04 pm (3rd ♏): Plant biennials, perennials, bulbs and roots. Prune. Irrigate. Fertilize (organic).

May 12, 10:28 am–May 13, 12:39 am (4th ♒): Cultivate. Destroy weeds and pests. Harvest fruits and root crops for food. Trim to retard growth.

May 19, 11:53 am–May 19, 2:48 pm (1st ♉): Plant annuals for hardiness. Trim to increase growth.

May 29, 10:51 am–May 31, 7:45 pm (2nd ♎): Plant annuals for fragrance and beauty. Trim to increase growth.

Set in Eastern Daylight Time (EDT)

Project Paperclip and NASA's Dark Past

At the end of World War II, US forces in Germany set about collecting captured Nazi technology, including items from their incredibly advanced rocket program. They soon realized, however, they would need the know-how of the men who designed them in order to assemble and understand the various components they had gathered. Thus, Project Paperclip was born. This secret operation selected a group of over 1,500 scientists, doctors, engineers, and technicians—all senior members of the Nazi party—and transferred them to the United States for employment in the government and military.

These men were rehabilitated with whitewashed backgrounds and slowly integrated into society. Many of these experts came from the Peenemünde Army Research Center, where the Nazis developed and manufactured their rocket program, including the world's first long-range ballistic missile, the V-2. Due to their advanced knowledge in the field, many were eventually put to work for America's newly established space agency, NASA, which was founded in 1958. Their work proved vital to the Apollo program.

The first director of the agency's Marshall Space Flight Center, in fact, was Wernher von Braun, former head of the Peenemünde operations. It must be noted, however, that von Braun and his fellow compatriots were not reluctant Nazis, no matter what their rewritten histories may suggest.

Set in Eastern Daylight Time (EDT)

May 2023

1 Monday

2nd ♍

☽ v/c 7:53 pm

Early May bank holiday (UK)

2 Tuesday

2nd ♍

☽ enters ♎ 2:09 am

3 Wednesday

2nd ♎

4 Thursday

2nd ♎

☽ v/c 5:17 am

☽ enters ♏ 10:32 am

Set in Eastern Daylight Time (EDT)

Friday 5

2nd ♏

Full Moon 1:34 pm

Cinco de Mayo

Lunar eclipse

Saturday 6

3rd ♏

☽ v/c 10:38 am

☽ enters ♐ 4:04 pm

Sunday 7

3rd ♐

	April								May								June				
S	M	T	W	T	F	S		S	M	T	W	T	F	S		S	M	T	W	T	F	S
						1			1	2	3	4	5	6						1	2	3
2	3	4	5	6	7	8		7	8	9	10	11	12	13		4	5	6	7	8	9	10
9	10	11	12	13	14	15		14	15	16	17	18	19	20		11	12	13	14	15	16	17
16	17	18	19	20	21	22		21	22	23	24	25	26	27		18	19	20	21	22	23	24
23	24	25	26	27	28	29		28	29	30	31					25	26	27	28	29	30	
30																					

May 2023

---

8 Monday

3rd ♐

☽ v/c 4:28 pm

☽ enters ♑ 7:33 pm

---

9 Tuesday

3rd ♑

---

10 Wednesday

3rd ♑

☽ v/c 7:52 pm

☽ enters ♒ 10:05 pm

---

11 Thursday

3rd ♒

Friday 12

3rd ≈≈

4th Quarter 10:28 am

☽ v/c 11:15 pm

Saturday 13

4th ≈≈

☽ enters ♓ 12:39 am

Sunday 14

4th ♓

☽ v/c 10:56 pm

Mother's Day

Mercury direct 11:17 pm

April						
S	M	T	W	T	F	S
						1
2	3	4	5	6	7	8
9	10	11	12	13	14	15
16	17	18	19	20	21	22
23	24	25	26	27	28	29
30						

May						
S	M	T	W	T	F	S
	1	2	3	4	5	6
7	8	9	10	11	12	13
14	15	16	17	18	19	20
21	22	23	24	25	26	27
28	29	30	31			

June						
S	M	T	W	T	F	S
				1	2	3
4	5	6	7	8	9	10
11	12	13	14	15	16	17
18	19	20	21	22	23	24
25	26	27	28	29	30	

May 2023

15 Monday
4th ♓
☽ enters ♈ 3:56 am

16 Tuesday
4th ♈

17 Wednesday
4th ♈
☽ v/c 5:10 am
☽ enters ♉ 8:28 am

18 Thursday
4th ♉

Set in Eastern Daylight Time (EDT)

Friday 19

4th ♉
New Moon 11:53 am
☽ v/c 1:51 pm
☽ enters ♊ 2:48 pm

Saturday 20

1st ♊

Sunday 21

1st ♊
☽ v/c 6:12 pm
☽ enters ♋ 11:28 pm

		April				
S	M	T	W	T	F	S
						1
2	3	4	5	6	7	8
9	10	11	12	13	14	15
16	17	18	19	20	21	22
23	24	25	26	27	28	29
30						

		May				
S	M	T	W	T	F	S
	1	2	3	4	5	6
7	8	9	10	11	12	13
14	15	16	17	18	19	20
21	22	23	24	25	26	27
28	29	30	31			

		June				
S	M	T	W	T	F	S
				1	2	3
4	5	6	7	8	9	10
11	12	13	14	15	16	17
18	19	20	21	22	23	24
25	26	27	28	29	30	

May 2023

22 Monday

1st ♋

Victoria Day (Canada)

23 Tuesday

1st ♋

24 Wednesday

1st ♋

☽ v/c 5:12 am

☽ enters ♌ 10:35 am

25 Thursday

1st ♌

Shavuot begins at sundown

Friday 26
1st ♌

☽ v/c 2:38 am

☽ enters ♍ 11:05 pm

Saturday 27
1st ♍

2nd Quarter 11:22 am

Sunday 28
2nd ♍

	April								May								June					
S	M	T	W	T	F	S		S	M	T	W	T	F	S		S	M	T	W	T	F	S
						1			1	2	3	4	5	6						1	2	3
2	3	4	5	6	7	8		7	8	9	10	11	12	13		4	5	6	7	8	9	10
9	10	11	12	13	14	15		14	15	16	17	18	19	20		11	12	13	14	15	16	17
16	17	18	19	20	21	22		21	22	23	24	25	26	27		18	19	20	21	22	23	24
23	24	25	26	27	28	29		28	29	30	31					25	26	27	28	29	30	
30																						

May 2023

29 Monday
2nd ♍
☽ v/c 5:46 am
☽ enters ♎ 10:51 am
Memorial Day
Spring bank holiday (UK)

30 Tuesday
2nd ♎

31 Wednesday
2nd ♎
☽ v/c 10:53 am
☽ enters ♏ 7:45 pm

Set in Eastern Daylight Time (EDT)

June

June 2023

Sun	Mon	Tue	Wed
4	5	6	7
11	12	13	14 Flag Day
● 18 Father's Day	19 Juneteenth	20	21
25	◑ 26	27	28
2	3	4	5

Set in Eastern Daylight Time (EDT)

Thu	Fri	Sat	
1	2	3 ○	*Notes*
8	9	10 ◑	
15	16	17	
22	23	24	
29	30	1	
6	7	8	

A Manned US Lunar Base: 1960s Style

In an era when the US government's defeatist attitude can't even figure out how to build a high-speed rail network, it is remarkable to witness the can-do spirit of American technicians of just a half-century ago—the same experts who landed man on the Moon in a mere seven years using primitive 1960s technology. They also drew up plans for a manned lunar base that is dazzling and dizzying in its ambitions. Released by the National Security Archive in 2014, the 1960 study, Project Horizon, laid out their vision for the first permanent, self-sustaining lunar colony, which could house twelve people at a time.

Once astronauts landed on the Moon and did preliminary explorations, construction would start immediately, including the immediate building of a nuclear reactor to provide a steady supply of energy. In order to feed the inhabitants, hydroponic agriculture would be used to grow salad greens, which would release enough oxygen so that chickens could be bred for meat and eggs. Algae would be used to grow fish and other aquatic life. If someone succumbed to the pressures of space life and experienced a psychotic break, the study's creators had the foresight to include an isolation chamber with external lock. Most remarkably, they felt the entire lunar station could be built and implemented in a mere five years.

---

1 Thursday

2nd ♏

Friday 2

2nd ♏

☽ v/c 8:51 pm

Coronation Day (UK)

Saturday 3

2nd ♏

☽ enters ♐ 1:03 am

Full Moon 11:42 pm

Sunday 4

3rd ♐

☽ v/c 11:24 pm

			May			
S	M	T	W	T	F	S
	1	2	3	4	5	6
7	8	9	10	11	12	13
14	15	16	17	18	19	20
21	22	23	24	25	26	27
28	29	30	31			

			June			
S	M	T	W	T	F	S
				1	2	3
4	5	6	7	8	9	10
11	12	13	14	15	16	17
18	19	20	21	22	23	24
25	26	27	28	29	30	

			July			
S	M	T	W	T	F	S
						1
2	3	4	5	6	7	8
9	10	11	12	13	14	15
16	17	18	19	20	21	22
23	24	25	26	27	28	29
30	31					

June 2023

5 Monday
3rd ♐

☽ enters ♑ 3:31 am

6 Tuesday
3rd ♑

7 Wednesday
3rd ♑

☽ v/c 12:40 am

☽ enters ♒ 4:42 am

8 Thursday
3rd ♒

Set in Eastern Daylight Time (EDT)

Friday 9

3rd ≈

☽ v/c 12:24 am

☽ enters ♓ 6:14 am

Saturday 10

3rd ♓

4th Quarter 3:31 pm

Sunday 11

4th ♓

☽ v/c 9:20 am

☽ enters ♈ 9:20 am

		May				
S	M	T	W	T	F	S
	1	2	3	4	5	6
7	8	9	10	11	12	13
14	15	16	17	18	19	20
21	22	23	24	25	26	27
28	29	30	31			

		June				
S	M	T	W	T	F	S
				1	2	3
4	5	6	7	8	9	10
11	12	13	14	15	16	17
18	19	20	21	22	23	24
25	26	27	28	29	30	

		July				
S	M	T	W	T	F	S
						1
2	3	4	5	6	7	8
9	10	11	12	13	14	15
16	17	18	19	20	21	22
23	24	25	26	27	28	29
30	31					

June 2023

12 Monday
4th ♈

13 Tuesday
4th ♈
☽ v/c 2:27 pm
☽ enters ♉ 2:31 pm

14 Wednesday
4th ♉
Flag Day

15 Thursday
4th ♉
☽ v/c 9:36 pm
☽ enters ♊ 9:46 pm

Set in Eastern Daylight Time (EDT)

Friday 16
4th ♊

Saturday 17
4th ♊

Sunday 18
4th ♊

New Moon 12:37 am

☽ v/c 2:24 am

☽ enters ♋ 6:58 am

Father's Day

		May								June								July			
S	M	T	W	T	F	S	S	M	T	W	T	F	S	S	M	T	W	T	F	S
	1	2	3	4	5	6					1	2	3							1
7	8	9	10	11	12	13	4	5	6	7	8	9	10	2	3	4	5	6	7	8
14	15	16	17	18	19	20	11	12	13	14	15	16	17	9	10	11	12	13	14	15
21	22	23	24	25	26	27	18	19	20	21	22	23	24	16	17	18	19	20	21	22
28	29	30	31				25	26	27	28	29	30		23	24	25	26	27	28	29
														30	31					

June 2023

19 Monday
1st ♋

Juneteenth

20 Tuesday
1st ♋

☽ v/c 5:43 pm

☽ enters ♌ 6:04 pm

21 Wednesday
1st ♌

Summer Solstice

22 Thursday
1st ♌

☽ v/c 1:01 pm

Set in Eastern Daylight Time (EDT)

Friday 23

1st ♌

☽ enters ♍ 6:35 am

Saturday 24

1st ♍

Sunday 25

1st ♍

☽ v/c 6:24 pm

☽ enters ♎ 6:57 pm

	May					
S	M	T	W	T	F	S
	1	2	3	4	5	6
7	8	9	10	11	12	13
14	15	16	17	18	19	20
21	22	23	24	25	26	27
28	29	30	31			

	June					
S	M	T	W	T	F	S
				1	2	3
4	5	6	7	8	9	10
11	12	13	14	15	16	17
18	19	20	21	22	23	24
25	26	27	28	29	30	

	July					
S	M	T	W	T	F	S
						1
2	3	4	5	6	7	8
9	10	11	12	13	14	15
16	17	18	19	20	21	22
23	24	25	26	27	28	29
30	31					

June 2023

26 Monday

1st ♎

2nd Quarter 3:50 am

27 Tuesday

2nd ♎

28 Wednesday

2nd ♎

☽ v/c 4:19 am

☽ enters ♏ 4:55 am

29 Thursday

2nd ♏

Friday 30

2nd ♏

☽ v/c 10:20 am

☽ enters ♐ 10:59 am

			May			
S	M	T	W	T	F	S
	1	2	3	4	5	6
7	8	9	10	11	12	13
14	15	16	17	18	19	20
21	22	23	24	25	26	27
28	29	30	31			

			June			
S	M	T	W	T	F	S
				1	2	3
4	5	6	7	8	9	10
11	12	13	14	15	16	17
18	19	20	21	22	23	24
25	26	27	28	29	30	

			July			
S	M	T	W	T	F	S
						1
2	3	4	5	6	7	8
9	10	11	12	13	14	15
16	17	18	19	20	21	22
23	24	25	26	27	28	29
30	31					

June's Moon at a Glance

June 3 Full Moon
Heal Thyself

At this time, moonlight is the best disinfectant. Go deep and thoroughly clean out all the nooks and crannies of your inner psyche. If you have been hesitant about trying counseling, this would be an excellent period to give it a go.

June 18 New Moon
Truth and Lies

This New Moon is demanding truth, but Neptune is covering things up with a nebulous coat of disinformation. While some deceptions may come to light, others may take hold. It is best to withhold your trust at this time until you can thoroughly vet things.

In the Garden

Jun. 3, 11:42 pm–Jun. 5, 3:31 am (3rd ♐): Cultivate. Destroy weeds and pests. Harvest fruits and root crops for food. Trim to retard growth.

Jun. 10, 3:31 pm–Jun. 11, 9:20 am (4th ♓): Plant biennials, perennials, bulbs and roots. Prune. Irrigate. Fertilize (organic).

Jun. 18, 6:58 am–Jun. 20, 6:04 pm (1st ♋): Plant grains, leafy annuals. Fertilize (chemical). Graft or bud plants. Irrigate. Trim to increase growth.

Jun. 26, 3:50 am–Jun. 28, 4:55 am (2nd ♎): Plant annuals for fragrance and beauty. Trim to increase growth.

July

July 2023

Sun	Mon	Tue	Wed
2	3 ○	4 Independence Day	5
9 ◑	10	11	12
16	17 ●	18	19
23	24	25 ◐	26
30	31	1	2

Set in Eastern Daylight Time (EDT)

Thu	Fri	Sat	Notes
		1	
6	7	8	
13	14	15	
20	21	22	
27	28	29	
3	4	5	

It's Only a Paper Moon

One of the more curious subgenres in the world of art is souvenir photography, which was popular in the United States from the late 1800s to mid-twentieth century. People attending fairs, carnivals, arcades, and other attractions would pay to get their picture taken and printed on a penny postcard. These items would be sent in the mail to loved ones or kept as a memento of the event. One of the most famous settings for these photos would be a crescent paper Moon.

This tradition served as the inspiration for the 1932 jazz standard "It's Only a Paper Moon," written by Harold Arlen with lyrics by Yip Harburg and Billy Rose, about a jaded man who finally finds true love. It was originally penned for the Ben Hecht and Gene Fowler Broadway play, *The Great Magoo*, but the show flopped, closing after only eleven performances. The tune, however, went on to become a cornerstone of the Great American Songbook, and various artists recorded their own renditions, such as Nat King Cole, Paul Whiteman, and Ella Fitzgerald, to name a few.

When director Peter Bogdanovich was considering *Paper Moon* (in reference to the song) as the title for his 1973 film about Depression-era America, he asked the advice of his mentor, Orson Welles. Welles exclaimed, "That title is so good, you shouldn't even make the picture, you should just release the title!" Bogdanovich had to add a scene where the protagonist gets her picture taken in a studio to get the name approved. The film went on to win an Academy Award for Tatum O'Neal as Best Supporting Actress.

In the Garden

Jul. 3, 7:39 am–Jul. 4, 1:30 pm (3rd ♑): Plant potatoes and tubers. Trim to retard growth.

Jul. 9, 9:48–Jul. 10, 7:55 pm (4th ♈): Cultivate. Destroy weeds and pests. Harvest fruits and root crops for food. Trim to retard growth.

Set in Eastern Daylight Time (EDT)

Jul. 17, 2:32 pm–Jul. 18, 12:39 am (1st ♋): Plant grains, leafy annuals. Fertilize (chemical). Graft or bud plants. Irrigate. Trim to increase growth.

Jul. 25, 6:07 pm–Jul. 27, 8:24 pm(2nd ♏): Plant grains, leafy annuals. Fertilize (chemical). Graft or bud plants. Irrigate. Trim to increase growth.

Saturday 1
2nd ♐

Canada Day

Sunday 2
2nd ♐

☽ v/c 9:33 am

☽ enters ♑ 1:20 pm

June							July							August					
S	M	T	W	T	F	S	S	M	T	W	T	F	S	S	M	T	W	T	F	S
				1	2	3							1			1	2	3	4	5
4	5	6	7	8	9	10	2	3	4	5	6	7	8	6	7	8	9	10	11	12
11	12	13	14	15	16	17	9	10	11	12	13	14	15	13	14	15	16	17	18	19
18	19	20	21	22	23	24	16	17	18	19	20	21	22	20	21	22	23	24	25	26
25	26	27	28	29	30		23	24	25	26	27	28	29	27	28	29	30	31		
							30	31												

July 2023

3 Monday

2nd \\$\\gamma$

Full Moon 7:39 am

4 Tuesday

3rd \\$\\gamma$

☽ v/c 12:45 pm

☽ enters ≈ 1:30 pm

Independence Day

5 Wednesday

3rd ≈

Tynwald Day (Isle of Man)

6 Thursday

3rd ≈

☽ v/c 9:42 am

☽ enters ♓ 1:33 pm

Friday 7

3rd ♓

Saturday 8

3rd ♓

☽ v/c 2:22 pm

☽ enters ♈ 3:19 pm

Sunday 9

3rd ♈

4th Quarter 9:48 pm

	June					
S	M	T	W	T	F	S
				1	2	3
4	5	6	7	8	9	10
11	12	13	14	15	16	17
18	19	20	21	22	23	24
25	26	27	28	29	30	

	July					
S	M	T	W	T	F	S
						1
2	3	4	5	6	7	8
9	10	11	12	13	14	15
16	17	18	19	20	21	22
23	24	25	26	27	28	29
30	31					

	August					
S	M	T	W	T	F	S
		1	2	3	4	5
6	7	8	9	10	11	12
13	14	15	16	17	18	19
20	21	22	23	24	25	26
27	28	29	30	31		

---

10 Monday

4th ♈︎

☽ v/c 7:11 pm

☽ enters ♉︎ 7:55 pm

---

11 Tuesday

4th ♉︎

---

12 Wednesday

4th ♉︎

Orangemen's Day (Northern Ireland)

---

13 Thursday

4th ♉︎

☽ v/c 2:11 am

☽ enters ♊︎ 3:26 am

Friday 14

4th ♊

Saturday 15

4th ♊

☽ v/c 8:35 am

☽ enters ♋ 1:13 pm

Sunday 16

4th ♋

	June					
S	M	T	W	T	F	S
				1	2	3
4	5	6	7	8	9	10
11	12	13	14	15	16	17
18	19	20	21	22	23	24
25	26	27	28	29	30	

	July					
S	M	T	W	T	F	S
						1
2	3	4	5	6	7	8
9	10	11	12	13	14	15
16	17	18	19	20	21	22
23	24	25	26	27	28	29
30	31					

	August					
S	M	T	W	T	F	S
		1	2	3	4	5
6	7	8	9	10	11	12
13	14	15	16	17	18	19
20	21	22	23	24	25	26
27	28	29	30	31		

July 2023

17 Monday
4th ♋

New Moon 2:32 pm

☽ v/c 11:06 pm

18 Tuesday
1st ♋

☽ enters ♌ 12:39 am

Islamic New Year begins at sundown

19 Wednesday
1st ♌

20 Thursday
1st ♌

☽ v/c 10:08 am

☽ enters ♍ 1:13 pm

Friday 21

1st ♍

Saturday 22

1st ♍

Sunday 23

1st ♍

☽ v/c 12:06 am

☽ enters ♎ 1:54 am

June						
S	M	T	W	T	F	S
				1	2	3
4	5	6	7	8	9	10
11	12	13	14	15	16	17
18	19	20	21	22	23	24
25	26	27	28	29	30	

July						
S	M	T	W	T	F	S
						1
2	3	4	5	6	7	8
9	10	11	12	13	14	15
16	17	18	19	20	21	22
23	24	25	26	27	28	29
30	31					

August						
S	M	T	W	T	F	S
		1	2	3	4	5
6	7	8	9	10	11	12
13	14	15	16	17	18	19
20	21	22	23	24	25	26
27	28	29	30	31		

Set in Eastern Daylight Time (EDT)

July 2023

---

24 Monday

1st ♎

---

25 Tuesday

1st ♎

☽ v/c 11:05 am

☽ enters ♏ 12:55 pm

2nd Quarter 6:07 pm

---

26 Wednesday

2nd ♏

---

27 Thursday

2nd ♏

☽ v/c 6:36 pm

☽ enters ♐ 8:24 pm

Set in Eastern Daylight Time (EDT)

Friday 28

2nd ♐

Saturday 29

2nd ♐

☽ v/c 7:51 pm

☽ enters ♑ 11:44 pm

Sunday 30

2nd ♑

	June					
S	M	T	W	T	F	S
				1	2	3
4	5	6	7	8	9	10
11	12	13	14	15	16	17
18	19	20	21	22	23	24
25	26	27	28	29	30	

	July					
S	M	T	W	T	F	S
						1
2	3	4	5	6	7	8
9	10	11	12	13	14	15
16	17	18	19	20	21	22
23	24	25	26	27	28	29
30	31					

	August					
S	M	T	W	T	F	S
		1	2	3	4	5
6	7	8	9	10	11	12
13	14	15	16	17	18	19
20	21	22	23	24	25	26
27	28	29	30	31		

31 Monday

2nd ♑
☽ v/c 10:13 pm
☽ enters ♒ 11:58 pm

July's Moon at a Glance

July 3 Full Moon/Supermoon

Follow Your Gut

This emotionally rich, nourishing Full Moon is urging us to turn off the judgments of the mind and let the compass of our soul be our guide. Learn to trust your instincts, as overly rational decision-making may be leading you in the wrong direction.

July 17 New Moon

The Fog of War

Everyone is jostling for power at this time, and instead of fighting fair, they will use any devious means at their disposable to get what they want. Before you get drawn into nonstop combat for someone else's cause, you may want to consider burning your draft card.

August

August 2023

Sun	Mon	Tue	Wed
		○ 1	2
6	7	◐ 8	9
13	14	15	● 16
20	21	22	23
27	28	29	○ 30
3	4	5	6

Set in Eastern Daylight Time (EDT)

Thu	Fri	Sat	Notes
3	4	5	
10	11	12	
17	18	19	
◑ 24	25	26	
31	1	2	
7	8	9	

Frau im Mond:
Fact Follows Fiction

In May's entry, we examined the ultimate fate of Nazi rocket scientists. But what about their beginnings? When German-Romanian doctoral student Hermann Oberth self-published his 1923 thesis as a book entitled *Die Rakete zu den Planetenräumen* (*The Rocket into Interplanetary Space*), Germany was rocked by rocket mania. This fad also captured the imagination of legendary German filmmaker Fritz Lang, who dedicated his final silent movie to a story about man traveling to the Moon, *Frau im Mond* (*Woman in the Moon*), and hired Oberth as its scientific advisor.

The 1929 film served to be quite prophetic, and many of its innovations were used in future space travel, including counting down to zero for liftoff; astronauts lying down during takeoff to withstand g-force pressure; the use of water on the launchpad to absorb the heat and sound of the engine; and a multistage rocket design that would detach certain components at various stages once in space. The film was very popular and went on to be one of the best-selling movies of the year. It also caught the eye of Nazi leadership, who saw a future in rocket technology—but as missiles, not spacecraft.

After World War I, the Treaty of Versailles severely limited the types of arms Germany could have in its arsenal. In 1933, the Nazis realized that rockets were not covered under these terms, so they created their V-2 rocket missile program, which was overseen by Oberth's devotee, Wernher von Braun, who went on to be a director at NASA and head of the Apollo space program. These young Nazi rocket scientists were so indebted to Oberth and Lang's vision that they placed the film's logo on their first successful V-2 rocket. The Nazis felt that Lang's movie was far too close to reality in its depiction of rocket technology and banned the film under their regime.

August's Moon at a Glance

August 1 Full Moon/Supermoon
Only You Can Prevent Forest Fires

With summer temperatures rising, any little spark could set off a major conflagration. Disasters can be prevented, however, by setting up strict boundaries and dousing your trigger spots with emotional fortitude when difficult people encroach upon your territory.

August 16 New Moon/Micromoon
Get Back Up

When you fall off a horse, rushing to the hospital may be better for the body, but remounting your steed and riding off into the sunset is definitely better for your inner spirit. This is a highly volatile Moon, but if you immediately face setbacks and anxieties, you will be able to master your emotions.

August 30 Full Moon/Supermoon/Blue Moon
Time Out

Follow the lead of the cooling temperatures and use the final days of summer to chill out and gather your thoughts. This is an excellent time to review the past few months and set out a strategy to reach your goals by the end of the year.

In the Garden

Aug. 1, 2:32 pm–Aug. 2, 11:05 pm (3rd ♒): Cultivate. Destroy weeds and pests. Harvest fruits and root crops for food. Trim to retard growth.

Aug. 8, 6:28 am–Aug. 9, 9:05 am (4th ♉): Plant potatoes and tubers. Trim to retard growth.

Aug. 19, 7:53 am–Aug. 21, 7:22 pm (1st ♎): Plant annuals for fragrance and beauty. Trim to increase growth.

August 2023

Aug. 26, 9:05 am–Aug. 28, 10:32 am (2nd ♑): Graft or bud plants. Trim to increase growth.

Aug. 30, 9:36 pm–Sep. 1, 9:25 am (3rd ♓): Plant biennials, perennials, bulbs and roots. Prune. Irrigate. Fertilize (organic).

---

1 Tuesday

2nd ♒

Full Moon 2:32 pm

---

2 Wednesday

3rd ♒

☽ v/c 5:15 pm

☽ enters ♓ 11:05 pm

---

3 Thursday

3rd ♓

Friday 4

3rd ♓

☽ v/c 9:21 pm

☽ enters ♈ 11:19 pm

Saturday 5

3rd ♈

Sunday 6

3rd ♈

	July					
S	M	T	W	T	F	S
						1
2	3	4	5	6	7	8
9	10	11	12	13	14	15
16	17	18	19	20	21	22
23	24	25	26	27	28	29
30	31					

	August					
S	M	T	W	T	F	S
		1	2	3	4	5
6	7	8	9	10	11	12
13	14	15	16	17	18	19
20	21	22	23	24	25	26
27	28	29	30	31		

	September					
S	M	T	W	T	F	S
					1	2
3	4	5	6	7	8	9
10	11	12	13	14	15	16
17	18	19	20	21	22	23
24	25	26	27	28	29	30

August 2023

7 Monday
3rd ♈
☽ v/c 12:13 am
☽ enters ♉ 2:25 am
Summer bank holiday (Scotland)

8 Tuesday
3rd ♉
4th Quarter 6:28 am

9 Wednesday
4th ♉
☽ v/c 6:39 am
☽ enters ♊ 9:05 am

10 Thursday
4th ♊

Friday 11

4th ♊

☽ v/c 1:27 pm

☽ enters ♋ 6:52 pm

Saturday 12

4th ♋

Sunday 13

4th ♋

	July							August							September					
S	M	T	W	T	F	S	S	M	T	W	T	F	S	S	M	T	W	T	F	S
						1		1	2	3	4	5							1	2
2	3	4	5	6	7	8	6	7	8	9	10	11	12	3	4	5	6	7	8	9
9	10	11	12	13	14	15	13	14	15	16	17	18	19	10	11	12	13	14	15	16
16	17	18	19	20	21	22	20	21	22	23	24	25	26	17	18	19	20	21	22	23
23	24	25	26	27	28	29	27	28	29	30	31			24	25	26	27	28	29	30
30	31																			

14 Monday

4th ♋

☽ v/c 3:46 am

☽ enters ♌ 6:36 am

15 Tuesday

4th ♌

16 Wednesday

4th ♌

☽ v/c 5:38 am

New Moon 5:38 am

☽ enters ♍ 7:14 pm

17 Thursday

1st ♍

Friday 18
1st ♍

Saturday 19
1st ♍
☽ v/c 4:51 am
☽ enters ♎ 7:53 am

Sunday 20
1st ♎

	July								August							September					
S	M	T	W	T	F	S		S	M	T	W	T	F	S		S	M	T	W	T	F	S
						1				1	2	3	4	5							1	2
2	3	4	5	6	7	8		6	7	8	9	10	11	12		3	4	5	6	7	8	9
9	10	11	12	13	14	15		13	14	15	16	17	18	19		10	11	12	13	14	15	16
16	17	18	19	20	21	22		20	21	22	23	24	25	26		17	18	19	20	21	22	23
23	24	25	26	27	28	29		27	28	29	30	31				24	25	26	27	28	29	30
30	31																					

August 2023

21 Monday

1st ♎︎

☽ v/c 4:31 pm

☽ enters ♏︎ 7:22 pm

22 Tuesday

1st ♏︎

23 Wednesday

1st ♏︎

Mercury retrograde 3:59 pm until 9/15

24 Thursday

1st ♏︎

☽ v/c 1:10 am

☽ enters ♐︎ 4:07 am

2nd Quarter 5:57 am

Set in Eastern Daylight Time (EDT)

Friday 25
2nd ♐

Saturday 26
2nd ♐
☽ v/c 7:56 am
☽ enters ♑ 9:05 am

Sunday 27
2nd ♑

		July								August								September				
S	M	T	W	T	F	S		S	M	T	W	T	F	S		S	M	T	W	T	F	S
						1				1	2	3	4	5							1	2
2	3	4	5	6	7	8		6	7	8	9	10	11	12		3	4	5	6	7	8	9
9	10	11	12	13	14	15		13	14	15	16	17	18	19		10	11	12	13	14	15	16
16	17	18	19	20	21	22		20	21	22	23	24	25	26		17	18	19	20	21	22	23
23	24	25	26	27	28	29		27	28	29	30	31				24	25	26	27	28	29	30
30	31																					

August 2023

28 Monday

2nd ♑

☽ v/c 7:49 am

☽ enters ♒ 10:32 am

Summer bank holiday (UK, except Scotland)

29 Tuesday

2nd ♒

☽ v/c 11:04 pm

30 Wednesday

2nd ♒

☽ enters ♓ 9:56 am

Full Moon 9:36 pm

31 Thursday

3rd ♓

Set in Eastern Daylight Time (EDT)

September

September 2023

Sun	Mon	Tue	Wed
3	4 Labor Day	5	◐ 6
10	11	12	13
17	18	19	20
24	25	26	27
1	2	3	4

Set in Eastern Daylight Time (EDT)

Thur	Fri	Sat	
	1	2	*Notes*
7	8	9	
● 14	15	16	
21	◐ 22	23	
28	○ 29	30	
5	6	7	

September's Moon at a Glance

September 14 New Moon Lunar Grand Trine

Off to a Great Start

The autumn season springs into gear with an incredibly productive New Moon creating an extremely auspicious lunar grand trine with a large number of heavy-hitting outer planets. All projects launched at this time will be born under these lucky vibes, so get cracking!

September 29 Full Moon/Supermoon

Moody Blues

The nights are getting longer and the universe is preparing for the winter ahead. It is time to say goodbye to the summer; energies are shifting from the extroverted vibes of the sunny season to a more low-key, cozier atmosphere.

Set in Eastern Daylight Time (EDT)

September 2023

Friday 1

3rd ♓

☽ v/c 6:36 am

☽ enters ♈ 9:25 am

Saturday 2

3rd ♈

Sunday 3

3rd ♈

☽ v/c 7:57 am

☽ enters ♉ 11:00 am

August						
S	M	T	W	T	F	S
		1	2	3	4	5
6	7	8	9	10	11	12
13	14	15	16	17	18	19
20	21	22	23	24	25	26
27	28	29	30	31		

September						
S	M	T	W	T	F	S
					1	2
3	4	5	6	7	8	9
10	11	12	13	14	15	16
17	18	19	20	21	22	23
24	25	26	27	28	29	30

October						
S	M	T	W	T	F	S
1	2	3	4	5	6	7
8	9	10	11	12	13	14
15	16	17	18	19	20	21
22	23	24	25	26	27	28
29	30	31				

September 2023

4 Monday
3rd ♉
Labor Day
Labour Day (Canada)

5 Tuesday
3rd ♉
☽ v/c 12:46 pm
☽ enters ♊ 4:07 pm

6 Wednesday
3rd ♊
4th Quarter 6:21 pm

7 Thursday
4th ♊
☽ v/c 6:22 pm

Set in Eastern Daylight Time (EDT)

Friday 8

4th ♊

☽ enters ♋ 1:00 am

Saturday 9

4th ♋

Sunday 10

4th ♋

☽ v/c 8:47 am

☽ enters ♌ 12:36 pm

	August					
S	M	T	W	T	F	S
		1	2	3	4	5
6	7	8	9	10	11	12
13	14	15	16	17	18	19
20	21	22	23	24	25	26
27	28	29	30	31		

	September					
S	M	T	W	T	F	S
					1	2
3	4	5	6	7	8	9
10	11	12	13	14	15	16
17	18	19	20	21	22	23
24	25	26	27	28	29	30

	October					
S	M	T	W	T	F	S
1	2	3	4	5	6	7
8	9	10	11	12	13	14
15	16	17	18	19	20	21
22	23	24	25	26	27	28
29	30	31				

September 2023

11 Monday
4th ♌

12 Tuesday
4th ♌
☽ v/c 11:06 am

13 Wednesday
4th ♌
☽ enters ♍ 1:18 am

14 Thursday
4th ♍
New Moon 9:40 pm

Friday 15

1st ♍

☽ v/c 9:49 am

☽ enters ♎ 1:44 pm

Rosh Hashanah begins at sundown

Mercury direct 4:21 pm

Saturday 16

1st ♎

Sunday 17

1st ♎

☽ v/c 9:06 pm

August						
S	M	T	W	T	F	S
		1	2	3	4	5
6	7	8	9	10	11	12
13	14	15	16	17	18	19
20	21	22	23	24	25	26
27	28	29	30	31		

September						
S	M	T	W	T	F	S
					1	2
3	4	5	6	7	8	9
10	11	12	13	14	15	16
17	18	19	20	21	22	23
24	25	26	27	28	29	30

October						
S	M	T	W	T	F	S
1	2	3	4	5	6	7
8	9	10	11	12	13	14
15	16	17	18	19	20	21
22	23	24	25	26	27	28
29	30	31				

18 Monday

1st

☽ enters ♏ 12:58 am

🍂 🐟

19 Tuesday

1st ♏

🍂 🐟

20 Wednesday

1st ♏

☽ v/c 6:21 am

☽ enters ♐ 10:06 am

21 Thursday

1st ♐

UN International Day of Peace

Friday 22

1st ✗

☽ v/c 3:32 pm

2nd Quarter 3:32 pm

☽ enters ♑ 4:20 pm

Saturday 23

2nd ♑

Fall Equinox

Sunday 24

2nd ♑

☽ v/c 4:05 pm

☽ enters ♒ 7:29 pm

Yom Kippur begins at sundown

	August					
S	M	T	W	T	F	S
		1	2	3	4	5
6	7	8	9	10	11	12
13	14	15	16	17	18	19
20	21	22	23	24	25	26
27	28	29	30	31		

	September					
S	M	T	W	T	F	S
					1	2
3	4	5	6	7	8	9
10	11	12	13	14	15	16
17	18	19	20	21	22	23
24	25	26	27	28	29	30

	October					
S	M	T	W	T	F	S
1	2	3	4	5	6	7
8	9	10	11	12	13	14
15	16	17	18	19	20	21
22	23	24	25	26	27	28
29	30	31				

September 2023

25 Monday
2nd ≈

26 Tuesday
2nd ≈
☽ v/c 8:38 am
☽ enters ♓ 8:18 pm

27 Wednesday
2nd ♓

28 Thursday
2nd ♓
☽ v/c 4:58 pm
☽ enters ♈ 8:17 pm

Friday 29

2nd ♈

Full Moon 5:58 am

Sukkot begins at sundown

Saturday 30

3rd ♈

☽ v/c 5:50 pm

☽ enters ♉ 9:18 pm

August						
S	M	T	W	T	F	S
		1	2	3	4	5
6	7	8	9	10	11	12
13	14	15	16	17	18	19
20	21	22	23	24	25	26
27	28	29	30	31		

September						
S	M	T	W	T	F	S
					1	2
3	4	5	6	7	8	9
10	11	12	13	14	15	16
17	18	19	20	21	22	23
24	25	26	27	28	29	30

October						
S	M	T	W	T	F	S
1	2	3	4	5	6	7
8	9	10	11	12	13	14
15	16	17	18	19	20	21
22	23	24	25	26	27	28
29	30	31				

The Moon Rock Hunters

It reads like something out of an adventurous television show: NASA has learned a vast number of its Moon rocks have gone missing. The lead investigator is also a college professor who enlists his students to help track them down. Only this isn't fiction—it's the true-life story of NASA Senior Special Agent Joseph Gutheinz, who has been chasing down these priceless objects for the past twenty years. Moon rocks are extremely rare. The six US Apollo missions brought back 2,196 rock samples, weighing a total of 842 pounds. The only other sources of lunar material on Earth were collected by Russian and Chinese rovers. Moon rocks also can be found in Antarctica and the desert regions of Africa and Oman, where they arrived as meteorites.

Their rarity makes them a target for black market collectors and thieves, but many Moon rocks were lost due to negligence, oversight, and bad record keeping. To commemorate the Apollo 11 and 17 missions, Richard Nixon gifted fragments of Moon rocks to all 50 states and 135 foreign governments; of these 270 "goodwill Moon rocks," 184 are missing. Their retrieval is Gutheinz and his students' mission, and altogether they have saved 78 rocks from the dustbin of history.

In the Garden

Sept. 6, 6:21 pm–Sept. 8, 1:00 am (4th ♊): Cultivate. Destroy weeds and pests. Harvest fruits and root crops for food. Trim to retard growth.

Sept. 15, 1:44 pm–Sept. 18, 12:58 am (1st ♎): Plant annuals for fragrance and beauty. Trim to increase growth.

Sept. 22, 4:20 pm–Sept. 24, 7:29 pm (2nd ♑): Graft or bud plants. Trim to increase growth.

Sept. 29, 5:58 am–Sept. 30, 9:18 pm (3rd ♈): Cultivate. Destroy weeds and pests. Harvest fruits and root crops for food. Trim to retard growth.

Set in Eastern Daylight Time (EDT)

October

October 2023

Sun	Mon	Tue	Wed
1	2	3	4
8	9	10	11
15	16	17	18
22	23	24	25
29	30	31 Halloween	1
5	6	7	8

Set in Eastern Daylight Time (EDT)

Thu	Fri	Sat	
5	6 ◑	7	*Notes*
12	13	14 ●	
19	20	21 ◐	
26	27	28 ○	
2	3	4	
9	10	11	

The Furry Friends Who Helped Put Us on the Moon

We all know the stories of the brave men and women who journeyed into space and onto the surface of the Moon, but what about the animals? Without the great sacrifices of our fellow earthly inhabitants, we could never have voyaged beyond the boundaries of our own landlocked existence. The first living organisms that were sent into space were fruit flies. These tiny insects share much genetic material with humans, making them excellent specimens for research. Next up was Albert II, the first monkey in space, who unfortunately died on impact due to parachute failure. Instead of monkeys, the Soviets were focusing on dogs, the most famous of whom was Laika, the first animal to orbit Earth. Originally, it was claimed that Laika perished due to running out of oxygen after about a week of her mission, but in 2002, the truth finally came out that she passed within hours of liftoff from overheating. The French favored cats, launching the first feline, Félicette, into space in 1963. While Félicette survived her flight, she was euthanized two months later so scientists could study the effects on her brain. Several other animals were launched in the early years of the space program to test the feasibility of life being blasted into space and returned to Earth unharmed, including frogs, rabbits, and mice.

October's Moon at a Glance

October 14 New Moon Annular Solar Eclipse

New World Order

It's time to stand up to the established powers that be in order to implement structural changes and build a better world for the future. While it may seem a daunting task, fighting for your visions today will allow them to take shape tomorrow. Don't be afraid to tear it all down and start anew.

October 28 Full Moon Partial Lunar Eclipse

Might Versus Right

Having virtue and justice on your side doesn't necessarily mean things will be smooth sailing. Crafty, duplicitous, warrior-like people are willing to do anything to get their way at this Full Moon. It's time to tap into your inner superhero and put a stop to their evil plans.

Sunday 1

3rd ♉

September						
S	M	T	W	T	F	S
					1	2
3	4	5	6	7	8	9
10	11	12	13	14	15	16
17	18	19	20	21	22	23
24	25	26	27	28	29	30

October						
S	M	T	W	T	F	S
1	2	3	4	5	6	7
8	9	10	11	12	13	14
15	16	17	18	19	20	21
22	23	24	25	26	27	28
29	30	31				

November						
S	M	T	W	T	F	S
			1	2	3	4
5	6	7	8	9	10	11
12	13	14	15	16	17	18
19	20	21	22	23	24	25
26	27	28	29	30		

October 2023

2 Monday

3rd ♉

☽ v/c 9:20 pm

3 Tuesday

3rd ♉

☽ enters ♊ 1:03 am

4 Wednesday

3rd ♊

5 Thursday

3rd ♊

☽ v/c 2:34 am

☽ enters ♋ 8:32 am

Set in Eastern Daylight Time (EDT)

Friday 6

3rd ♋
4th Quarter 9:48 am
Sukkot ends

Saturday 7

4th ♋
☽ v/c 3:12 pm
☽ enters ♌ 7:24 pm

Sunday 8

4th ♌

September						
S	M	T	W	T	F	S
					1	2
3	4	5	6	7	8	9
10	11	12	13	14	15	16
17	18	19	20	21	22	23
24	25	26	27	28	29	30

October						
S	M	T	W	T	F	S
1	2	3	4	5	6	7
8	9	10	11	12	13	14
15	16	17	18	19	20	21
22	23	24	25	26	27	28
29	30	31				

November						
S	M	T	W	T	F	S
			1	2	3	4
5	6	7	8	9	10	11
12	13	14	15	16	17	18
19	20	21	22	23	24	25
26	27	28	29	30		

9 Monday
4th ♌

Indigenous Peoples' Day

Thanksgiving Day (Canada)

10 Tuesday
4th ♌

☽ v/c 5:37 am

☽ enters ♍ 8:02 am

11 Wednesday
4th ♍

12 Thursday
4th ♍

☽ v/c 4:10 pm

☽ enters ♎ 8:22 pm

Friday 13

4th ♎

Saturday 14

4th ♎

New Moon 1:55 pm

Solar eclipse

Sunday 15

1st ♎

☽ v/c 3:01 am

☽ enters ♏ 7:04 am

September								October								November						
S	M	T	W	T	F	S		S	M	T	W	T	F	S		S	M	T	W	T	F	S
					1	2		1	2	3	4	5	6	7					1	2	3	4
3	4	5	6	7	8	9		8	9	10	11	12	13	14		5	6	7	8	9	10	11
10	11	12	13	14	15	16		15	16	17	18	19	20	21		12	13	14	15	16	17	18
17	18	19	20	21	22	23		22	23	24	25	26	27	28		19	20	21	22	23	24	25
24	25	26	27	28	29	30		29	30	31						26	27	28	29	30		

October 2023

16 Monday
1st ♏

17 Tuesday
1st ♏
☽ v/c 11:44 am
☽ enters ♐ 3:36 pm

18 Wednesday
1st ♐

19 Thursday
1st ♐
☽ v/c 3:02 pm
☽ enters ♑ 9:55 pm

Set in Eastern Daylight Time (EDT)

Friday 20
1st ♑

Saturday 21
1st ♑

2nd Quarter 11:29 pm

Sunday 22
2nd ♑

☽ v/c 2:00 am

☽ enters ♒ 2:06 am

September						
S	M	T	W	T	F	S
					1	2
3	4	5	6	7	8	9
10	11	12	13	14	15	16
17	18	19	20	21	22	23
24	25	26	27	28	29	30

October						
S	M	T	W	T	F	S
1	2	3	4	5	6	7
8	9	10	11	12	13	14
15	16	17	18	19	20	21
22	23	24	25	26	27	28
29	30	31				

November						
S	M	T	W	T	F	S
			1	2	3	4
5	6	7	8	9	10	11
12	13	14	15	16	17	18
19	20	21	22	23	24	25
26	27	28	29	30		

October 2023

23 Monday
2nd ≈

☽ v/c 3:04 pm

24 Tuesday
2nd ≈

☽ enters ♓ 4:33 am

25 Wednesday
2nd ♓

26 Thursday
2nd ♓

☽ v/c 2:39 am

☽ enters ♈ 6:02 am

Set in Eastern Daylight Time (EDT)

Friday 27

2nd ♈

Saturday 28

2nd ♈

☽ v/c 4:20 am

☽ enters ♉ 7:44 am

Full Moon 4:24 pm

Lunar eclipse

Sunday 29

3rd ♉

British Summer Time ends at 2 am

September						
S	M	T	W	T	F	S
					1	2
3	4	5	6	7	8	9
10	11	12	13	14	15	16
17	18	19	20	21	22	23
24	25	26	27	28	29	30

October						
S	M	T	W	T	F	S
1	2	3	4	5	6	7
8	9	10	11	12	13	14
15	16	17	18	19	20	21
22	23	24	25	26	27	28
29	30	31				

November						
S	M	T	W	T	F	S
			1	2	3	4
5	6	7	8	9	10	11
12	13	14	15	16	17	18
19	20	21	22	23	24	25
26	27	28	29	30		

30 Monday

3rd ♉

☽ v/c 7:36 am

☽ enters ♊ 11:08 am

31 Tuesday

3rd ♊

Halloween

In the Garden

Oct. 6, 9:48 am–Oct. 7, 7:24 pm (4th ♋): Plant biennials, perennials, bulbs and roots. Prune. Irrigate. Fertilize (organic).

Oct. 14, 1:55 pm–Oct. 15, 7:04 am (1st ♎): Plant annuals for fragrance and beauty. Trim to increase growth.

Oct. 21, 11:29 pm–Oct. 22, 2:06 am (2nd ♑): Graft or bud plants. Trim to increase growth.

Oct. 28, 4:24 pm –Oct. 30, 11:08 am (3rd ♉): Plant potatoes and tubers. Trim to retard growth.

November

November 2023

Sun	Mon	Tue	Wed
			1
◑ 5 Daylight Saving Time ends	6	7 Election Day (general)	8
12	● 13	14	15
19	◐ 20	21	22
26	○ 27	28	29
3	4	5	6

Thu	Fri	Sat	
2	3	4	*Notes*
9	10	11 Veterans Day	
16	17	18	
23 Thanksgiving Day	24	25	
30	1	2	
7	8	9	

Drawing Down the Moon

In most Neopagan, Witchcraft, and Wiccan traditions, the Moon is seen as a representative of the goddess, with its energy being the brightest and most powerful during a Full Moon. Drawing Down the Moon is a ceremony that taps into the nourishing strength of this luminous force, where a high priestess or individual invites the Moon to inhabit their vessel. This can be done alone, in a circle, or with the assistance of a high priest. Once the goddess has descended into the body, the priestess then enters a trancelike state, allowing the goddess to communicate directly with other members present through a back-and-forth dialogue or a monologue.

The ritual starts by the priestess opening their arms at the Full Moon and reciting an evocation, such as Doreen Valiente's "The Charge of the Goddess." Many prayers, chants, and mantras can be found online for use in this rite, or the practitioner could speak spontaneously in their own words. Drawing Down the Moon is a powerful, advanced technique that takes a large amount of concentration and practice. Ordinary individuals can also perform this ritual as a means of replenishing and sharing their energy with the universe, healing, and letting go of negative energies, fears, and doubts. Prepare for this event by eating only healthy, unprocessed foods and taking a cleansing bath before the ritual.

Set in Eastern Daylight Time (EDT)

November's Moon at a Glance

November 13 New Moon

Running to Stay in Place

This month, the cosmic treadmill is operating at warp speed, bringing an onslaught of incessant change that would put even the most superhuman powers to the test. Luckily, this Moon is also bursting with energy and stamina, allowing you to face all challenges with courage and determination.

November 27 Full Moon

The True Meaning of Power

This Moon pits the forces of sheer control against self-actualization. It is time to stop trying to achieve goals by influencing and holding sway over others, and replace this toxic approach with action and self-reliance. Only by placing the locus of power within ourselves, instead of the others around us, can we ever become the true masters of our destiny.

In the Garden

Nov. 5, 3:37 am–Nov. 6, 2:39 pm (4th ♌): Cultivate. Destroy weeds and pests. Harvest fruits and root crops for food. Trim to retard growth.

Nov. 13, 4:27 am–Nov. 13, 9:23 am (1st ♏): Plant grains, leafy annuals. Fertilize (chemical). Graft or bud plants. Irrigate. Trim to increase growth.

Nov. 20, 9:29 am–Nov. 22, 12:19 pm (2nd ♓): Plant grains, leafy annuals. Fertilize (chemical). Graft or bud plants. Irrigate. Trim to increase growth.

Nov. 27, 4:16 am–Nov. 29, 1:54 am (3rd ♊): Cultivate. Destroy weeds and pests. Harvest fruits and root crops for food. Trim to retard growth.

---

1 Wednesday

3rd ♊

☽ v/c 8:36 am

☽ enters ♋ 5:30 pm

All Saints' Day

---

2 Thursday

3rd ♋

Friday 3

3rd ♋

☽ v/c 11:28 pm

Saturday 4

3rd ♋

☽ enters ♌ 3:21 am

Sunday 5

3rd ♌

4th Quarter 3:37 am

Daylight Saving Time ends at 2 am

Bonfire Night (UK)

	October							November							December					
S	M	T	W	T	F	S	S	M	T	W	T	F	S	S	M	T	W	T	F	S
1	2	3	4	5	6	7				1	2	3	4						1	2
8	9	10	11	12	13	14	5	6	7	8	9	10	11	3	4	5	6	7	8	9
15	16	17	18	19	20	21	12	13	14	15	16	17	18	10	11	12	13	14	15	16
22	23	24	25	26	27	28	19	20	21	22	23	24	25	17	18	19	20	21	22	23
29	30	31					26	27	28	29	30			24	25	26	27	28	29	30
														31						

November 2023

6 Monday
4th ♌
☽ v/c 2:25 am
☽ enters ♍ 2:39 pm

7 Tuesday
4th ♍
Election Day (general)

8 Wednesday
4th ♍
☽ v/c 11:55 pm

9 Thursday
4th ♍
☽ enters ♎ 3:08 am

Friday 10

4th ♎

Saturday 11

4th ♎

☽ v/c 10:05 am

☽ enters ♏ 1:39 pm

Veterans Day

Remembrance Day (Canada)

Sunday 12

4th ♏

	October							November							December					
S	M	T	W	T	F	S	S	M	T	W	T	F	S	S	M	T	W	T	F	S
1	2	3	4	5	6	7				1	2	3	4						1	2
8	9	10	11	12	13	14	5	6	7	8	9	10	11	3	4	5	6	7	8	9
15	16	17	18	19	20	21	12	13	14	15	16	17	18	10	11	12	13	14	15	16
22	23	24	25	26	27	28	19	20	21	22	23	24	25	17	18	19	20	21	22	23
29	30	31					26	27	28	29	30			24	25	26	27	28	29	30
														31						

November 2023

13 Monday
4th ♏

New Moon 4:27 am

☽ v/c 6:03 pm

☽ enters ♐ 9:23 pm

14 Tuesday
1st ♐

15 Wednesday
1st ♐

☽ v/c 5:57 pm

16 Thursday
1st ♐

☽ enters ♑ 2:41 am

Friday 17

1st ♑

Saturday 18

1st ♑

☽ v/c 3:27 am

☽ enters ♒ 6:28 am

Sunday 19

1st ♒

October						
S	M	T	W	T	F	S
1	2	3	4	5	6	7
8	9	10	11	12	13	14
15	16	17	18	19	20	21
22	23	24	25	26	27	28
29	30	31				

November						
S	M	T	W	T	F	S
			1	2	3	4
5	6	7	8	9	10	11
12	13	14	15	16	17	18
19	20	21	22	23	24	25
26	27	28	29	30		

December						
S	M	T	W	T	F	S
					1	2
3	4	5	6	7	8	9
10	11	12	13	14	15	16
17	18	19	20	21	22	23
24	25	26	27	28	29	30
31						

November 2023

20 Monday

1st ♒

☽ v/c 5:50 am

2nd Quarter 5:50 am

☽ enters ♓ 9:29 am

21 Tuesday

2nd ♓

22 Wednesday

2nd ♓

☽ v/c 10:10 am

☽ enters ♈ 12:19 pm

23 Thursday

2nd ♈

Thanksgiving Day

Friday 24

2nd ♈

☽ v/c 12:40 pm

☽ enters ♉ 3:29 pm

Saturday 25

2nd ♉

Sunday 26

2nd ♉

☽ v/c 4:52 pm

☽ enters ♊ 7:40 pm

October						
S	M	T	W	T	F	S
1	2	3	4	5	6	7
8	9	10	11	12	13	14
15	16	17	18	19	20	21
22	23	24	25	26	27	28
29	30	31				

November						
S	M	T	W	T	F	S
			1	2	3	4
5	6	7	8	9	10	11
12	13	14	15	16	17	18
19	20	21	22	23	24	25
26	27	28	29	30		

December						
S	M	T	W	T	F	S
					1	2
3	4	5	6	7	8	9
10	11	12	13	14	15	16
17	18	19	20	21	22	23
24	25	26	27	28	29	30
31						

November 2023

27 Monday
2nd ♊

Full Moon 4:16 am

28 Tuesday
3rd ♊

☽ v/c 8:03 pm

29 Wednesday
3rd ♊

☽ enters ♋ 1:54 am

30 Thursday
3rd ♋

St. Andrew's Day (Scotland)

December

December 2023

Sun	Mon	Tue	Wed
3	4	◐ 5	6
10	11	● 12	13
17	18	◑ 19	20
24 Christmas Eve	25 Christmas Day	○ 26	27
31 New Year's Eve	1	2	3

Thu	Fri	Sat	Notes
	1	2	_____
			_____
			_____
7	8	9	_____
			_____
			_____
14	15	16	_____
			_____
			_____
21	22	23	_____
			_____
			_____
28	29	30	_____
			_____
			_____
4	5	6	_____
			_____

Set in Eastern Standard Time (EST)

Close Encounters in Outer Space

From Roswell to Rendlesham, the world is well aware of the numerous accounts of UFOs spotted from Earth. Surely, astronauts would have their own sightings to share, yet there have been surprisingly few personal accounts of unidentified lights or objects being witnessed in the vastness of space, and almost all can be attributed to jettisoned parts of the spacecraft or booster-associated debris.

One of the most famous quotes regarding UFOs in outer space was made by the second man to walk on the Moon, Buzz Aldrin, during an appearance in a 2005 documentary for the Science Channel. His statements certainly generated a lot of buzz, but, unfortunately, they were taken completely out of context. He started off by describing a time when he saw lights outside of the window of the Apollo 11 craft that seemed to be following them, and finished by saying "technically" it could be considered as unidentified. The filmmakers, however, intentionally cut out the part where Aldrin explains they were probably seeing sunlight reflecting off the panels that had separated from the aircraft. Subsequent rumors floated around the internet erroneously stating that Aldrin had taken a lie detector test proving he had seen aliens. In reality, however, the nebulous-sounding Institute of BioAccoustic Biology and Sound Health had merely analyzed recordings of Aldrin from decades ago and stated that they found the tone of his voice contradicted the words he was actually saying—in other words, bunk science.

Set in Eastern Standard Time (EST)

Friday 1
3rd ♋
☽ v/c 8:07 am
☽ enters ♌ 11:00 am

Saturday 2
3rd ♌

Sunday 3
3rd ♌
☽ v/c 9:11 pm
☽ enters ♍ 10:50 pm

		November								December								January '24			
S	M	T	W	T	F	S		S	M	T	W	T	F	S		S	M	T	W	T	F	S
			1	2	3	4							1	2			1	2	3	4	5	6
5	6	7	8	9	10	11		3	4	5	6	7	8	9		7	8	9	10	11	12	13
12	13	14	15	16	17	18		10	11	12	13	14	15	16		14	15	16	17	18	19	20
19	20	21	22	23	24	25		17	18	19	20	21	22	23		21	22	23	24	25	26	27
26	27	28	29	30				24	25	26	27	28	29	30		28	29	30	31			
								31														

December 2023

---

4 Monday

3rd ♍

---

5 Tuesday

3rd ♍

4th Quarter 12:49 am

---

6 Wednesday

4th ♍

☽ v/c 8:50 am

☽ enters ♎ 11:35 am

---

7 Thursday

4th ♎

Hanukkah begins at sundown

Friday 8

4th ♎︎

☽ v/c 8:05 pm

☽ enters ♏︎ 10:35 pm

Saturday 9

4th ♏︎

Sunday 10

4th ♏︎

November								December								January '24					
S	M	T	W	T	F	S		S	M	T	W	T	F	S		S	M	T	W	T	F	S
			1	2	3	4							1	2			1	2	3	4	5	6
5	6	7	8	9	10	11		3	4	5	6	7	8	9		7	8	9	10	11	12	13
12	13	14	15	16	17	18		10	11	12	13	14	15	16		14	15	16	17	18	19	20
19	20	21	22	23	24	25		17	18	19	20	21	22	23		21	22	23	24	25	26	27
26	27	28	29	30				24	25	26	27	28	29	30		28	29	30	31			
								31														

December 2023

11 Monday

4th ♏

☽ v/c 3:57 am

☽ enters ♐ 6:11 am

12 Tuesday

4th ♐

New Moon 6:32 pm

13 Wednesday

1st ♐

☽ v/c 1:48 am

☽ enters ♑ 10:31 am

Mercury retrograde 2:09 am until 1/1/24

14 Thursday

1st ♑

Friday 15

1st ♑

☽ v/c 11:04 am

☽ enters ♒ 12:56 pm

Hanukkah ends

Saturday 16

1st ♒

Sunday 17

1st ♒

☽ v/c 7:04 am

☽ enters ♓ 2:58 pm

November						
S	M	T	W	T	F	S
			1	2	3	4
5	6	7	8	9	10	11
12	13	14	15	16	17	18
19	20	21	22	23	24	25
26	27	28	29	30		

December						
S	M	T	W	T	F	S
					1	2
3	4	5	6	7	8	9
10	11	12	13	14	15	16
17	18	19	20	21	22	23
24	25	26	27	28	29	30
31						

January '24						
S	M	T	W	T	F	S
	1	2	3	4	5	6
7	8	9	10	11	12	13
14	15	16	17	18	19	20
21	22	23	24	25	26	27
28	29	30	31			

December 2023

---

18 Monday

1st ♓

---

19 Tuesday

1st ♓

2nd Quarter 1:39 pm

☽ v/c 4:03 pm

☽ enters ♈ 5:47 pm

---

20 Wednesday

2nd ♈

---

21 Thursday

2nd ♈

☽ v/c 9:47 pm

☽ enters ♉ 9:50 pm

Winter Solstice

Set in Eastern Standard Time (EST)

December 2023

Friday 22

2nd ♉

Saturday 23

2nd ♉

Sunday 24

2nd ♉

☽ v/c 1:40 am

☽ enters ♊ 3:15 am

Christmas Eve

November						
S	M	T	W	T	F	S
			1	2	3	4
5	6	7	8	9	10	11
12	13	14	15	16	17	18
19	20	21	22	23	24	25
26	27	28	29	30		

December						
S	M	T	W	T	F	S
					1	2
3	4	5	6	7	8	9
10	11	12	13	14	15	16
17	18	19	20	21	22	23
24	25	26	27	28	29	30
31						

January '24						
S	M	T	W	T	F	S
	1	2	3	4	5	6
7	8	9	10	11	12	13
14	15	16	17	18	19	20
21	22	23	24	25	26	27
28	29	30	31			

December 2023

---

25 Monday

2nd ♊

Christmas Day

---

26 Tuesday

2nd ♊

☽ v/c 2:55 am

☽ enters ♋ 10:15 am

Full Moon 7:33 pm

Kwanzaa begins (ends Jan. 1)

Boxing Day (Canada & UK)

---

27 Wednesday

3rd ♋

---

28 Thursday

3rd ♋

☽ v/c 5:57 pm

☽ enters ♌ 7:23 pm

Friday 29
3rd ♌

Saturday 30
3rd ♌

Sunday 31
3rd ♌

☽ v/c 12:18 am

☽ enters ♍ 6:53 am

New Year's Eve

November						
S	M	T	W	T	F	S
			1	2	3	4
5	6	7	8	9	10	11
12	13	14	15	16	17	18
19	20	21	22	23	24	25
26	27	28	29	30		

December						
S	M	T	W	T	F	S
					1	2
3	4	5	6	7	8	9
10	11	12	13	14	15	16
17	18	19	20	21	22	23
24	25	26	27	28	29	30
31						

January '24						
S	M	T	W	T	F	S
	1	2	3	4	5	6
7	8	9	10	11	12	13
14	15	16	17	18	19	20
21	22	23	24	25	26	27
28	29	30	31			

December's Moon at a Glance

December 12 New Moon

No Time for Foolishness

Bring a perfect end to the year by weeding out all the manipulators, grifters, and emotional vampires from your world. It is time to invest your energies and efforts into improving your own life and going after your personal goals instead of having your inner force rerouted to enhancing the dreams of others.

December 26 Full Moon

Time to Clean Up the Christmas Wrappings

Christmas is over. It's time to clean up the open boxes and put away your presents. This is a great time to organize your closet and your life; a sense of emotional and intellectual clarity can be achieved by decluttering the world around you.

In the Garden

Dec. 5, 12:49 am–Dec. 6, 11:35 am (4th ♍): Cultivate, especially medicinal plants. Destroy weeds and pests. Trim to retard growth.
Dec. 13, 10:31 am–Dec. 15, 12:56 pm (1st ♑): Graft or bud plants. Trim to increase growth.
Dec. 19, 1:39 pm–Dec. 19, 5:47 pm (2nd ♓): Plant grains, leafy annuals. Fertilize (chemical). Graft or bud plants. Irrigate. Trim to increase growth.
Dec. 26, 7:33 pm–Dec. 28, 7:23 pm (3rd ♋): Plant biennials, perennials, bulbs and roots. Prune. Irrigate. Fertilize (organic).

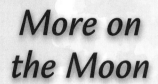

More on the Moon

The Eight Phases of the Moon

By Amy Herring

As Earth orbits the Sun, the Moon orbits Earth, reflecting the Sun's light back to us. The Sun is always lighting the side of the Moon that faces it, but we don't always see the illuminated side as the Moon circles us approximately monthly. Over the course of about fourteen nights, the light of the Moon waxes, growing more full as each night passes, until a seemingly perfect circle shines in the heavens. Then the Moon's light begins to visibly wane, returning over another fourteen nights to darkness until the Moon's light diminishes entirely. The Moon is dark once more until the cycle begins again. This cycle repeats about every twenty-nine days.

As the saying goes, "As above, so below." The waxing and waning of the Moon is a symbol of life itself, ingrained into human consciousness. Just as we are born, grow, and die, the Moon seems to do so as well. We can tap into this lunar symbolism by aligning our intentions and actions with the energy of the current lunar phase.

During the waxing half of the lunar cycle, the light is growing and expanding, symbolizing a good time for things here on Earth to expand and grow as well. It's a good time to plant and nurture seeds, to set plans in motion, and act on our desires. There is a sense of things building.

During the waning half of the lunar cycle, the light is diminishing, symbolizing a time to reap what we've sown, and to review, let go, and surrender. It is a good time to release things that have run their course and close doors that have stood open too long. Near the end of the waning phases, we can cleanse and prepare for the renewal of the cycle.

The Lunar Phases

While this light cycle of the Moon is continuous and unbroken, eight lunar phases offer a way to mark the transitions in the shape of the Moon's reflected light during its monthly cycle. The phases are typically known as the new, waxing crescent, first quarter, waxing gibbous, full, waning gibbous, third quarter, and waning crescent phases.

The Moon's entry into each of these phases is not necessarily as exact as the chime of a clock striking the hour; in fact, four of these phases mark a threshold and the other four represent the journey toward the next threshold. The four crescent and gibbous phases (both waxing and waning) are not moments in time but periods between the thresholds when the Moon could be said to be "crescenting" or "gibbous-ing" as it makes its way from new to full and back to new again.

Finding the Moon

Just like the Sun appears to rise and set, so does the Moon, rising and setting about an hour later each day as it moves around the Earth in its orbit. In its waxing phase, it is often too close to the Sun to see properly until after the Sun has set. As it gets further along in its cycle of phases, its position in the sky is more distant from the Sun, making it easier to see for longer periods of time, even sometimes during the daylight hours.

The Moon's light always grows from right to left in the northern hemisphere, and left to right in the southern hemisphere. It is delightfully simple to recognize whether the Moon is waxing or waning just by sight—just give yourself a "hand." Hold your right hand up to the Moon. If the curve of your hand between your index finger and thumb corresponds to the curve of the light side of the Moon, the Moon is waxing. If it's the opposite, the Moon is waning, and the curve of the light side of the Moon will correspond to your open left hand instead. In the southern hemisphere, this is reversed—simply switch hands to perform this lunar magic trick!

The Phases

New Moon (Dark Moon)

 The Moon cannot be seen in the sky when in its new phase. The lit side of the Moon faces away from us, and the night sky is illuminated only by starlight. A New Moon rises and sets in relative unison with the Sun, too close to it to be seen.

The phases of the Moon represent a never-ending cycle, but the period of the New Moon is often considered the beginning, the renewal, of this cycle, and it is a good time for your own beginnings, to act on what you've been planning or to try something new. This is a time for experimentation and spontaneity.

This phase is sometimes referred to as a dark Moon (for obvious reasons). During this phase, there is no guiding light on the path. This is a phase of instinct, a time when we must feel our way forward. It is a good time to try something new or take a step in a good direction, even if you don't know where it will lead. The New Moon is a time to act on things that are meant to grow, like a seed being planted. Hope and enthusiasm, even if seemingly naïve, are the attitudes to embrace.

If you were born during a New Moon phase, you are learning to trust what you know inside and act on it with faith in your inner guidance system, even if you don't always end up where you'd hoped you would.

Waxing Crescent Moon

 As the light of the Moon moves from total darkness to the balance of light and dark at the first quarter phase, a crescent of light grows. The waxing crescent Moon is an early riser, getting up just after sunrise. This Moon is difficult to see during the day but look to the west to see her just after sunset. The farther along from the New Moon phase, the easier it is to spot the Moon in this phase.

Both the new and waxing crescent phases of the Moon have a feeling of spring about them—the enthusiasm of bursting into the world and a sense of being at the beginning of something just starting to get underway. The seed that was planted now begins to push a tiny sprout above the soil.

A sense of momentum is present in this phase, as the growing light gains more ground each night. It is a good time to seek out sources of inspiration and support to keep up the projects or goals you've begun and continue to put forth an enthusiastic effort.

If you were born during a waxing crescent Moon, you are deeply in tune with potential and possibility and may feel most nourished when you are able to express your heart through a sense of mission or purpose. You are learning how to follow through on the things that matter most over time.

First Quarter Moon

At the first quarter Moon, the waxing light appears balanced: half of the face of the Moon lies in darkness and half is illuminated. This Moon can be easily seen moving through the sky for most of the day, setting in the west around midnight.

A sense of anticipation prevails during this phase. The seed has now grown beyond just a small sprout but has not yet produced blossoms.

This threshold is a tipping point. From here until the Full Moon phase, the scales will tip toward the light side, like spring expanding into summer. It is not uncommon to experience bumps in the road, and this phase is a good time to confront obstacles and acknowledge conflicts to work past any stalled energy. In the previous phase, you needed to build momentum; here, you need courage and conviction to continue moving forward. You may feel like you have something to prove, although possibly only to yourself.

If you were born during this phase, you are likely to fight for what you feel is important rather than live in complacency but may struggle with overconfidence and impatience.

Waxing Gibbous Moon

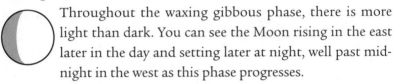

Throughout the waxing gibbous phase, there is more light than dark. You can see the Moon rising in the east later in the day and setting later at night, well past midnight in the west as this phase progresses.

After the make-or-break, confrontational feeling of the first quarter Moon, a sense of promise embodies this phase. Now the seed has grown into a plant and is beginning to sprout buds—there is no need to prove yourself because the result, though not fully grown, can start to speak for itself.

This is a good time to seek out assistance from those who can reinforce your confidence in yourself and the goals and projects you have undertaken. This can also be a social time where a sense of collaboration, formal or informal, is most beneficial. This is still a waxing phase so there is still something building, but the angst and fervor present in the earlier phases is more relaxed now. It's a good time for activities that require patience, continued effort, and some fine-tuning.

If you were born under a waxing gibbous Moon, you may find you have an instinct for supporting and connecting with others on many levels, not because you are necessarily an extrovert, but that you have a knack for collaboration and bringing ideas and people together.

Full Moon

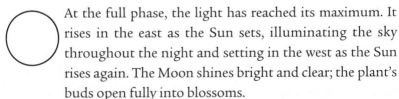

At the full phase, the light has reached its maximum. It rises in the east as the Sun sets, illuminating the sky throughout the night and setting in the west as the Sun rises again. The Moon shines bright and clear; the plant's buds open fully into blossoms.

If you have something to reveal or express, now can be a good time to do so, even if you are not sure you are ready. Share, socialize, and let the world see what you are and hear what you have to say.

There may be a sense of exposure during this phase. It can seem that everything is running at high power when the Moon is full, including our emotions. Whatever has been brewing and building now manifests; for good or ill, it comes into full view.

It is common for things to feel like they are coming to a head during this time, or something not previously seen is now in full view. The Full Moon can bring revelations, even if there isn't necessarily understanding or clarity.

None of us are perfect, but if you were born during the full phase, you are meant to lay all your beauty out bare to the world, ready or not. You are learning to be comfortable with your humanness and foibles and not let embarrassment, fear, or shame hold you back from your sincerest expression of self.

Waning Gibbous (Disseminating) Moon

The light from the Full Moon is now waning, with the Moon rising later each day after sunset and setting in the west after dawn.

In this "afterglow" phase just past the Full Moon, the light begins to wane, the blossoms becoming overripe and drooping under their own weight. This lunar phase is sometimes called the disseminating phase, symbolizing a time to share what you've learned and gather feedback from others. Recently completed projects, especially of a creative nature, may feel like they are taking on a life of their own.

You may have an intuitive sense of things beginning to come to an end. The fast, building pace of the waxing phases can feel too manic in the waning phases. It is a time to review what is working, what has worked, and what's no longer working. Seek some objectivity and distance if a situation has been dominating your time or emotions. If things have been culminating, there may be a sense of letdown that might be simultaneously a relief on some level, depending on your feelings about the outcome.

If you were born under this phase, you may have the heart of the philosopher or teacher, with a desire to share a message or bring others to clarity. You are learning to let go of how others receive your message and simply find fulfillment in giving and wisdom.

Last (Third/Reconciling) Quarter Moon

The face of the Moon is once again divided down the center, a moment of balance before giving way to the growing dark. The Moon rises in the east near midnight during this phase and sets in the west well after sunrise.

This threshold is a good time to break through stalled energy by confronting and releasing anything that needs to be let go. This Moon is sometimes called a reconciling Moon, symbolizing a good time to take stock and see if we are holding on to anything—be it circumstances, objects, or relationships—that has already run its course, and to wrap things up and put things in order.

The plant that has long since flowered and produced fruit is now ready to die and return to the earth, but it cannot if we cling to it or prop it up. If something in you or a situation you are in is ready to collapse and give way to change, this phase is a good time to acknowledge fears that may be standing in the way. Acknowledge what you intuitively see coming. Releasing feelings of sorrow and surrendering to the natural course can ultimately bring relief.

This phase is also a good time to begin to consolidate our energy, to draw energy inward rather than expel it outward. Save money rather than spend, use what you have rather than acquire something new; the beginning of this phase may carry more angst but reflection, meditation, and rest are in alignment with this phase as it progresses farther toward the crescent.

If you were born during this phase, you may feel caught between two instincts: the instinct to engage with the world, share your wisdom, make things happen, fight the good fight, and the instinct to disengage. You may be a bit of a nonconformist by default as you strive to keep the balance between living in the world but not being a product of it.

Waning Crescent (Balsamic) Moon

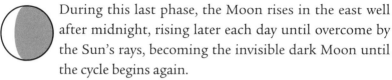 During this last phase, the Moon rises in the east well after midnight, rising later each day until overcome by the Sun's rays, becoming the invisible dark Moon until the cycle begins again.

This phase symbolizes a time of both restoration and preparation. There is a feeling of finality to this phase and it's a good time to tie up loose ends, finish what has been started where possible, and banish what you wish to see ended. Practically speaking, this is a good time for cutting ties or breaking bad habits.

This last lunar phase is sometimes referred to as balsamic, a word whose origins refer to a substance used to heal wounds and soothe pains. The energy of this phase is best utilized in rest, solitude, and simplicity, to heal and regroup, if needed.

The previous waning phases lead us ever more toward a path's end. As this phase progresses, we may start to sense the promise of renewal around the bend. It is a good time to clear the way in preparation for new insights and actions, but do not rush. Now is a time for meditation, hibernation, and patience as new insights and plans make their way into your consciousness.

If you were born during a balsamic Moon, you may be constantly in tune with the inevitability of life, consciously or unconsciously. You are challenged with living to the fullest while always being aware of a sense of finality. You possess an inner mystic that can reveal wisdom beyond your years, but you may also struggle with melancholy and be prone to nostalgia.

And the cycle begins again.

World Time Zones

Compared to Eastern Standard Time

(R)	EST (used here)	(D)	Add 9 hours
(S)	CST/Subtract 1 hour	(D*)	Add 9.5 hours
(Q)	Add 1 hour	(E)	Add 10 hours
(P)	Add 2 hours	(E*)	Add 10.5 hours
(O)	Add 3 hours	(F)	Add 11 hours
(Z)	Add 5 hours	(F*)	Add 11.5 hours
(T)	MST/Subtract 2 hours	(G)	Add 12 hours
(U)	PST/Subtract 3 hours	(H)	Add 13 hours
(U*)	Subtract 3.5 hours	(I)	Add 14 hours
(V)	Subtract 4 hours	(I*)	Add 14.5 hours
(V*)	Subtract 4.5 hours	(K)	Add 15 hours
(W)	Subtract 5 hours	(K*)	Add 15.5 hours
(X)	Subtract 6 hours	(L)	Add 16 hours
(Y)	Subtract 7 hours	(L*)	Add 16.5 hours
(A)	Add 6 hours	(M)	Add 17 hours
(B)	Add 7 hours	(M*)	Add 18 hours
(C)	Add 8 hours	(P*)	Add 2.5 hours
(C*)	Add 8.5 hours		

Eastern Standard Time = Universal Time (Greenwich Mean Time) + or − the value from the table.

World Map of Time Zones

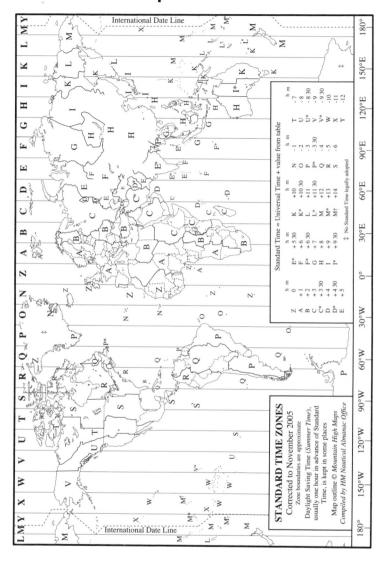

International Date Line

Standard Time = Universal Time + value from table

	h m		h m
Z	0	K	+10
A	+1	K*	+10.30
B	+2	L	+11
C	+3	L*	+11.30
C*	+3.30	M	+12
D	+4	M*	+13
D*	+4.30	M†	+14
E	+5		
E*	+5.30	N	-1
F	+6	O	-2
F*	+6.30	P	-3
G	+7	P*	-3.30
H	+8	Q	-4
I	+9	R	-5
I*	+9.30	S	-6
		T	-7
		U	-8
		U*	-8.30
		V	-9
		V*	-9.30
		W	-10
		X	-11
		Y	-12

† No Standard Time legally adopted

STANDARD TIME ZONES

Corrected to November 2005

Zone boundaries are approximate

Daylight Saving Time (*Summer Time*), usually one hour in advance of Standard Time, is kept in some places

Map outline © *Mountain High Maps*
Compiled by HM Nautical Almanac Office

International Date Line

Get in Tune with the Moon's Spirited Energy

A bestseller since 1905, Llewellyn's *Moon Sign Book* has helped millions take advantage of the moon's dynamic energies. With lunar timing tips on planting and harvesting and a guide to companion plants, this popular guide is also a gardener's best friend. Use this essential life-planning tool to choose the best dates for almost anything: getting married, buying or selling your home, requesting a promotion, applying for a loan, traveling, having surgery, seeing the dentist, picking mushrooms, and much more.

LLEWELLYN'S MOON SIGN BOOK

320 pp. • 5¼ × 8

978-0-7387-6397-2 • U.S. $13.99 CAN $19.99

To order call 1-877-NEW-WRLD

www.llewellyn.com